About the Author

L iz Palika has been writing professionally since 1985, when she was first published in *Dog Fancy* magazine. Since then she has written more than fifty books and more than a thousand magazine articles and columns. She has been published in *Dog World*, *Cats*, *Cat Fancy*, *AKC Gazette*, and other pet publications, as well as *Newsweek*, *The Saturday Evening Post*, and *Women First*. Her books include *The KISS Guide to Raising a Puppy*, *The Ultimate Dog Treat Cookbook*, *The Ultimate Cat Treat Cookbook*, and *All Dogs Need Some Training*.

Palika's books have been awarded many honors. *Australian Shepherd: Champion of Versatility* won Best Breed Book from the Dog Writers Association of America (DWAA) and Best Nonfiction Book from the San Diego Book Writers. *Save That Dog!* won Best General Reference Book from the DWAA and the first ASPCA Pet Overpopulation Answers Award. Palika's work has also won awards from the Cat Writers' Association and Purina, as well as others from the DWAA. Palika was honored with the San Diego Leadership Award; she was named a North County Woman of Merit; and in 2005 she was awarded the DWAA's Distinguished Service Award.

Palika has been teaching dogs and their owners in North County, San Diego for almost twenty-five years. A former member of the National Association of Dog Obedience Instructors (NADOI) and founding member of the Association of Pet Dog Trainers (APDT), Palika is also a charter member of the International Association of Canine Professionals (IACP) and is a Certified Dog Trainer (CDT) through this organization. She is also American Kennel Club Canine Good Citizen (AKCCGC) Evaluator #4182.

Working in Vista, California (San Diego County), Palika trains over a thousand dogs and their families a year and has put obedience titles on over twenty dogs of her own, from Doberman pinschers to papillons, in addition to her beloved Australian shepherds.

Praise for *The Ultimate Pet Food Guide*

"Finally, a book that arms concerned pet owners with understandable, easy-to-implement nutritional choices . . . Will reading *The Ultimate Pet Food Guide* save your pet's life? Perhaps. Will Palika's nutritional analysis and advice empower you to give your pet better nutrition and a healthier life? Most certainly. *Your pet is what he eats.* He needs a pet nutrition-savvy owner to control his diet and protect his nutritional well-being."

—Sarah Ferrell, author of *Devoted To Dogs:*
How To Be Your Dog's Best Owner

THE
ULTIMATE
PET FOOD GUIDE

Also by Liz Palika . . . .

The Howell Book of Dogs

The KISS Guide to Raising a Puppy

The Pocket Idiot's Guide to Housetraining

And many more. For more on Liz's books go to www.lizpalika.com.

THE

ULTIMATE

PET FOOD GUIDE

Everything You Need to Know
about Feeding Your Dog or Cat

LIZ PALIKA

Da Capo

LIFE
LONG

A Member of the Perseus Books Group

Designed by Trish Wilkinson
Set in 11.5 point Goudy

Cataloging-in-Publication data for this book is available from the Library of Congress.

First Da Capo Press edition 2008
ISBN 978-1-60094-071-2

Published by Da Capo Press
A Member of the Perseus Books Group
www.dacapopress.com

Note: The information in this book is true and complete to the best of our knowledge. This book is intended only as an informative guide for those wishing to know more about health issues. In no way is this book intended to replace, countermand, or conflict with the advice given to you by your own veterinarian. The ultimate decision concerning care should be made between you and your pet's doctor. We strongly recommend you follow his or her advice. Information in this book is general and is offered with no guarantees on the part of the authors of Da Capo Press. The authors and publisher disclaim all liability in connection with the use of this book.

Da Capo Press books are available at special discounts for bulk purchases in the United States by corporations, institutions, and other organizations. For more information, please contact the Special Markets Department at the Perseus Books Group, 2300 Chestnut Street, Suite 200, Philadelphia, PA 19103, or call (800) 255-1514, or e-mail special.markets@perseusbooks.com.

1 2 3 4 5 6 7 8 9

Contents

Introduction

Early in 2007, after thousands of pets suddenly became seriously ill, pet owners began bringing their cats and dogs to their respective veterinarians, and the animals began dying, mostly due to kidney failure. When all the clues were put together, fingers began pointing toward Canadian pet-food manufacturer Menu Foods, which was manufacturing foods sold under hundreds of pet-food labels.

In mid-March 2007 the FDA issued the recall of 60 million cans and pouches of dog and cat foods made by Menu Foods, containing wheat gluten that had been imported from China. That wheat gluten, which is used to help formed pet-food product keep its shape and to increase the protein level of the food, was tainted with melamine. Melamine is used in making plastic.

This, unfortunately, was just the beginning of a huge fiasco. There were additional recalls, which continue even as this book is being written. Corn gluten has also been recalled, as has rice gluten. As consumer awareness has increased and additional testing has been done, other toxins have been found in the foods and additives.

More than six thousand pets are known to have fallen ill during this episode, and more than three thousand have died, although complete figures will probably never be known. Some pets may have died prior to the news breaking of the problem, and many veterinarians were too busy treating admitted pets to report deaths to the FDA.

If there is any good to be created of this incident, it is the awareness that pet owners now have of the importance of good, clean foods for their pet. Although I hate the idea of anyone's pet dying, especially in such a horrible way, if these pets' lives can save others, perhaps there is some good to be found in it.

I became very aware of the importance of pet nutrition many years ago when my German shepherd dogs were prone to gastrointestinal upsets. Due to their needs, I began studying pet nutrition with the guidance and support of the veterinarians I worked for. This came into good play several years ago when the Australian shepherd belonging to my husband and I, Dax, was diagnosed with a serious liver disorder at the age of six.

Copper toxicosis is a disease in which copper, an essential mineral, builds up in the liver until it reaches toxic proportions. The disease is common in Bedlington terriers, there is no cure, and those who have it rarely live beyond the age of seven or eight years. Upon Dax's diagnosis, I decided to try and help support her through nutrition, since there was no medical cure, and I'm happy to say Dax just celebrated her thirteenth birthday. She still has copper toxicosis, but her diet is helping her liver cope.

Along the way, I have seen exactly how much food affects the quality of our pets' lives:

- The food that is eaten affects the animal's body condition and state of health.
- Food and diet are important to the health of the immune system and can affect how an animal develops a disease or disorder, and how the animal recuperates from it.
- The food that is eaten provides the animal with energy, and a poor diet leaves the animal unable to work, play, or exercise hard.
- Food sources are important. Plants grown in mineral-poor soils will not nourish the animal, and poor-quality cuts of meats will not supply good proteins or fats.
- As a dog trainer today, I also see the relationship food has with canine behavior.
- And much, much more.

Now, years after I began studying pet nutrition, my interest in it continues; this is my seventh book on pet foods. After the pet-food recalls in 2007, I found myself answering thousands of questions from concerned dog and cat owners, and I realized this book was desperately needed.

So please, read and reread. Make notes, copy recipes, and try the recipes. Your dogs and cats will thank you!

Liz Palika
And my canine companions:
Dax (thirteen years old), Riker (eight years old),
and Bashir (three years old)
And my feline companions:
Havoc (seventeen years old), Xena (nine years old),
Pumpkin, and Squash (two years old).

CHAPTER ONE

The Digestive System of Dogs and Cats

What We Feed Them Does Matter

You have probably thought about your digestive tract—people usually do every once in a while—especially if your digestive tract has reacted badly to a food you ate. But when all is going well and the body is healthy, we tend to take things for granted.

But have you ever wondered about your pet's inner workings? Before we talk about dog and cat foods, we need to have at least a basic understanding of how our pets' digestive systems function. Below, you'll learn about the similarities our digestive systems share, as well as our differences, especially in regard to cats. In addition, we'll take a look at some of the problems that can bother the digestive system and warning signs so you can tell when your pet is in distress.

The Digestive Process

Digestion is the process where the food is changed, both chemically and physically, and is made ready for absorption. These changes take place in the digestive tract, which begins in the mouth and finishes when the wastes are excreted as urine and feces.

Food is taken in through the mouth, and in people, digestion begins here as food is chewed. The enzyme ptyalin is secreted by the salivary glands, and thus begins the digestive process, even before the food is swallowed. The foods are well chewed so the person doesn't choke and so the enzyme can actually begin its work; if large pieces of food are swallowed, the enzyme will not be as efficient. In addition, chewing helps break up plant matter (cellulose) so that the plant nutrients can be digested later.

But there is actually another early step, predigestion, that is important. What is your favorite food? A tri-tip steak cooked on the grill? Served with sautéed onions? Or would you prefer a hot fudge sundae with whipped cream and nuts? In any case, when you think about a favorite food, your mind recalls the smell and taste of it. Then, when you see the food and when you smell it, your digestive juices start flowing, both the saliva in your mouth and gastric juices in your stomach. This is predigestion, and it is an aid to the digestive process.

The same applies with dogs and cats. If food that is unappealing is offered, less saliva and fewer gastric juices are released. As a result, fewer enzymes begin to work on the food. Susan Donoghue, VMD, the nutritional columnist for the American Kennel Club's *AKC Gazette* magazine, says, "Gastric predigestion can be improved by adding palatable, highly digestible foods to the animal's diet."

Taste Preferences

Like people, dogs and cats have taste buds on the tongue; however, what appeals to each species varies somewhat. People, in general, are attracted to foods high in salt or sugar. Many dogs enjoy sugar too—and can get addicted to it just as people can—but are also attracted to meat and fat. Cats do not have the taste receptors for sugar, and most appear more attracted to meat and fat.

The Teeth and Jaws

Dogs and cats both have teeth designed to procure foods. Dogs have forty-two teeth that are strong and sharp and backed by powerful jaw muscles. Wild canines use these teeth and muscles to grab and hang on to prey animals, and then to rip the meat off in chunks that can be swallowed. The small cats, who have thirty teeth, are obviously not as powerful as most hunting canines and do not have the large teeth and jaw muscles that dogs have. However, even a domestic house cat's teeth are sharp and meant for hunting. Their teeth also aid in shearing the meat off the prey animal. Although both dogs and cats do chew their food, they do so significantly less thoroughly than people do, and the chewing plays a much smaller part in their digestive process.

Jocelynn Jacobs, DVM, author of *Performance Dog Nutrition* (Sno Shire Publications, 2005) says, "Another important function of the mouth is producing saliva. Saliva is 99 percent water; the remaining 1 percent is mucus, inorganic salts and enzymes."

The mucus is important, as it coats the food so that it can be more easily swallowed.

The Gastrointestinal Tract

When food is swallowed, it travels through the esophagus to the stomach. The esophagus is a long muscular tube that uses peristalsis (involuntary wavelike motions) to move the food to the stomach.

Although digestion begins in the mouth for people, it begins in the stomach for dogs and cats. The stomach holds the food and adds digestive enzymes and acids. Once the food in the stomach mixes with all of the gastric juices, it is the consistency of a thick, lumpy paste and is called chyme.

The small intestine is a narrow, coiled organ in the abdomen. It is vital to the digestion of food; this is where proteins complete their transformation into amino acids and peptides, where fatty acids are produced from fats, and where glucose is produced from carbohydrates. The small intestine is lined with small projections called villi, which make the walls of the intestine look like it has thousands of tiny fingers. These small formations provide significantly more absorption area for the small intestine, as each is covered with nutrient-absorbing material. The nutrients are taken in by the villi, move into their tiny blood vessels, and then continue into the bloodstream. They are carried to the liver, which filters out harmful substances and portions out nutrients, some of which are sent to the cells to be used immediately and some of which are saved by the liver for future use. Vitamins and minerals are also absorbed in the small intestine.

The large intestine does not contain any villi; instead the walls are smooth. The large intestine absorbs water and any

People, Dogs, and Cats

• •

The small intestine in humans is about twenty feet long. This length is necessary so that all the foods people normally eat can be digested, from meats and fats to a variety of plant materials.

In a dog, the small intestine is usually five times the dog's body length, so a dog who is 25 inches long would have a small intestine that is 125 inches long. Dogs, although technically called carnivores, can also eat and digest some other foods, including a few fruits and plant materials.

Cats are true carnivores, however, and are not equipped (through teeth and digestive enzymes) to eat plant materials. Therefore, they have a significantly shorter intestine that is designed solely to digest meats and fats.

electrolytes that are remaining from the material moving through it. When healthy, it also has a flourishing bacterial population. These bacteria aid in digesting any fibers that have been ingested, and any protein, fats, or carbohydrates that have not yet been digested. As the food moves through the large intestine, it becomes drier and more compact, until it reaches the rectum and is excreted as feces.

Eating (and Digestion) Is Life

Food is necessary for a number of different things—all of which are vital for life. The macronutrients—protein, fat, and carbohydrates—are required in varying amounts, depending upon the species. Dogs and cats both need proteins, which are important for growth, for repair and maintenance, and for the formation of hormones. Proteins are the source of essential amino acids and enzymes in the body. Fats are vital for the absorption of the fat-soluble vitamins and provide a source of necessary fatty acids. Fat is also an easily used source of energy. Carbohydrates are another source of energy and help with the digestion of other foods. Although both dogs and cats have dietary requirements for protein and fat, cats have no nutritional need for carbohydrates.

The micronutrients are needed in smaller quantities than the macronutrients but are just as essential. The micronutrients include vitamins and minerals, most of which have more than one function, but work as coenzymes in the body. Phytochemicals are micronutrients from plants, most of which act as powerful antioxidants. All of these, the macro- and micronutrients, will be discussed in more detail in the next chapter.

The immune system keeps your dog or cat healthy, and that also requires good nutrition. All immune systems (human, canine, or feline) are dependant upon the consumption and absorption of a number of macro- and micronutrients, including zinc. But most importantly your immune system needs foods rich in natural enzymes.

Life Stages Affect Digestion

Many things can affect nutrition and digestion, including the age and the stage of life of your pet. This requires your pet's diet to change, and also how he may react to specific foods, how well those foods are digested, and the results the foods produce will change.

Kittens and puppies, for example, nurse for their first few weeks of life, and most mother cats and dogs are able to do that. The fat, roly-poly kittens and puppies are then, traditionally, weaned to a commercial kitten or puppy food. Although some babies will do well on these foods, others fail to thrive and need something else. Jocelynn Jacobs, DVM, said, "Young puppies and active youngsters have quick intestinal speeds, often preventing proper absorption of nutrients." These puppies (and kittens) usually need multiple nutrient-rich meals throughout the day.

Hardworking dogs, performance sport dogs, and active young cats may also, with their increased activity levels, move foods through the digestive system too quickly. Dr. Jacobs said that it's important for even hardworking and very active animals to get a chance to rest. These rest periods will help slow the digestive process slightly, so that the animal can absorb the nutrients in the food that it has eaten.

Senior dogs and cats often have problems absorbing all of the nutrients from their foods. These dogs and cats become thin, with poor coats and a lack of muscle tone. These animals would do better on a nutrient-rich diet made from ingredients that are easier to digest. The special needs of puppies and kittens, active adults, and older pets will be discussed in more detail in upcoming chapters. In later chapters you'll also find recipes tailored for special-needs pets.

Digestive Tract Disorders

The digestive system is a complicated and essential part of a living animal. When it is working right, digesting food well, adding nutrients to the body's cells, and excreting wastes, it is a work of art. However, when something goes wrong, things can go horribly wrong. Upsets and diseases of the gastrointestinal tract can be uncomfortable, painful, disruptive, create breaks in house-training, and can sometimes even be fatal.

Unfortunately, many things can disrupt the gastrointestinal tract. A course of antibiotics for a problem unrelated to the digestive tract can wipe out the bacterial colony in the large intestine, thereby causing upsets there, including diarrhea. Eating grass in the backyard, chewing up and swallowing pieces of a toy, a bacterial infection, or catching a virus can all cause problems.

Listed below are some serious (or potentially serious) gastrointestinal problems, including their symptoms, and problems that can be caused by or be made worse by poor nutrition. However, this listing is for your education as a pet owner and is not designed to replace your veterinarian. If you're concerned your dog or cat has a problem, call your veterinarian.

Vomiting

This is the process by which food is forced from the stomach back up the esophagus and out the mouth. Cats sometimes seem to vomit more than most dogs, especially if the cat throws up hair balls (from hair swallowed during grooming). Dogs and cats both may vomit if the stomach is upset, either from the food that has been eaten or from illness or other factors, including poisoning.

If the dog or cat vomits once and there is hair in the vomit, or grass, or something that was swallowed that shouldn't have been, the animal is probably fine. Just don't offer food or water for a couple of hours. However, if the vomiting is repetitive and violent, then the veterinarian needs to be called. If the vomiting continues for more than one day, the veterinarian should definitely be consulted.

Diarrhea

Loose, soft stools are often the result of an irritation or imbalance in the large intestine. This can be caused by the food the dog or cat has eaten, or the treats consumed, or it can be caused by illness.

If the dog has two or three bouts of diarrhea during the day but otherwise appears to be fine, just withhold food for a few hours, allowing the dog to drink, and let his system calm itself. Diarrhea that is severe, continues for more than twenty-four hours, or has blood in it can also be a symptom of a more serious illness, and the veterinarian should be called.

Cats can dehydrate more rapidly than do most dogs and so diarrhea needs to be taken more seriously. If your cat has one or two incidences of diarrhea during one day, call your veterinarian for guidance.

Urinary Tract Disease

Dogs and cats both can have urinary tract problems that can range from inflammation and infections to stones in the kidneys or bladder. There are many potential causes of these problems, from an inherited tendency to poor nutrition. If your dog or cat is straining to urinate, is urinating more often, or has blood in the urine, call your veterinarian right away.

Kidney Disease

Many dogs and cats develop kidney disease as a part of the aging process. Unfortunately, the stress of eating a poor diet for years can exacerbate the problem, especially in cats who may not drink enough water to keep the system well flushed and the kidneys working correctly. Always make sure your dog or cat has clean, fresh drinking water available.

Symptoms of kidney disease include the following:

- increased urination
- increased thirst
- loss of appetite and weight loss
- loss of house-training or litter-box skills
- foul breath
- vomiting and diarrhea

You will need your veterinarian's assistance to support your pet if he or she does have kidney disease. With good care and nutrition, many pets can live for quite a long time with kidney disease.

Dental Disease

Dental problems are one of the most common pet-health issues today. While some sources state that dry dog and cat foods will help keep teeth clean, that hasn't been proven, and even if it were true, that wouldn't be sufficient dental care. Dogs and cats both need regular dental care. The teeth should be cleaned at home at least twice a week (your veterinarian can show you how) and at the vet's clinic at least yearly. In addition, your pet needs good nutritious foods to support good dental health.

Bloat and Torsion

Bloat is more common in large, deep-chested dogs, but it can happen in any dog if the conditions are right. There is suspected to be a genetic relationship between dogs and bloat, but that is still being researched. It has been seen more often in Great Danes, Saint Bernards, German shepherds, Labrador retrievers, golden retrievers, bullmastiffs, mastiffs, and bulldogs.

Cats, luckily, have escaped this potentially fatal ailment. Although cats can have flatulence, their stomachs don't swell and turn as dogs' stomachs can.

When a dog bloats, the stomach enlarges. This usually happens when the dog has eaten and has quite a bit of water in the stomach, and gases are released by the food. If the stomach is greatly enlarged or overly full, it can even twist and turn (called torsion). In doing so, it closes off any avenue for fluids, foods, or gases to escape from the stomach. The affected dog can easily suffer from shock and die unless veterinary care is obtained immediately.

Symptoms of bloat include the following:

- pacing, restlessness, looking at the stomach, and even biting at the abdominal area
- a swollen abdomen
- more than normal gas, including burping
- attempting to vomit, dry heaves, and drooling
- a vacant, staring expression in the eyes

Although research is still continuing, most experts recommend feeding a dog prone to bloat a high-quality diet, skipping those low-quality foods that produce gases, especially soy-based foods. The dog should be fed more than one meal a day and should refrain from strenuous exercise for at least an hour or two after eating.

Inflammatory Bowel Disease (IBD)

IBD is a chronic inflammatory condition. It can be a reaction to certain foods or chemicals or additives in the foods, or it can be inherited. Rottweilers, golden retrievers, German shepherds, and Irish setters are more prone to IBD than other breeds.

Cats have also been known to develop IBD, although an inherited tendency in cats is not yet known and no specific cat breeds have seemed to have developed an inherited tendency toward this ailment.

Symptoms may include the following:

- vomiting
- soft stool or diarrhea
- blood in the feces
- abdominal spasms

Over time, the dog or cat will lose weight, can become dehydrated, and will fail to thrive. Veterinary care is needed to help manage IBD. In addition, a good-quality diet free of artificial colorings, flavorings, preservatives, and other additives is needed. For dogs, a homemade diet that consists of 40 percent meat, 50 percent wild or brown rice, and 10 percent steamed vegetables will usually calm the system. Cats should eat 70 percent meat, 20 percent rice, and 10 percent steamed vegetables. This diet can continue until the system is stabilized.

Megaesophagus

When food moves down the esophagus from the mouth to the stomach, it does so with wavelike motions called peristalsis. When those motions do not happen as they should, food can back up or collect in the esophagus, causing the food to be regurgitated or to stall in the esophagus. When this happens regularly, the esophagus can become enlarged.

Megaesophagus can be a congenital defect (present at birth) or it can occur later in life. It can also be symptomatic of other problems. Although this can occur in dogs and cats, it is seen more often in dogs. It is known to be an inherited defect in wire fox terriers and miniature schnauzers, and has been seen in German shepherds, Newfoundlands, Great Danes, pugs, and greyhounds.

This is not seen as often in cats as it is in dogs, and there doesn't seem to be any relation as to breeds of cats.

Symptoms include the following:

- regurgitation of undigested (just swallowed) food
- cough and nasal discharge (from vomiting)
- difficultly swallowing or discomfort after swallowing
- weight loss and poor body condition

This condition should be monitored by a veterinarian, as it can have drastic effects on your pet's health, from malnutrition and starvation to pneumonia from aspirated vomit. The veterinarian will also provide feeding guidelines for your dog or cat. He may recommend that your pet eat a very soft diet that will be easy to swallow, and that he should eat from an elevated (elbow height) bowl.

Megacolon

Megacolon is a problem with the large intestine. Moving through the large intestine, the food stalls at some point, usually down near the rectum, and the dog or cat is not able to defecate.

As the animal continues to eat, additional mass accumulates in the large intestine. Constipation results, and the colon becomes stretched and enlarged, often leading to a chronic condition.

Although seen in both dogs and cats, it is more common in cats, although one individual breed does not seem to develop it more often than any other. Megacolon can be a congenital defect, but it can also happen later in life. There can be many causes of this condition, from the cat not wanting to use a dirty litter box to an incorrect diet.

Symptoms can include the following:

- very small pieces of stool
- less frequent defecation
- straining to defecate
- lack of appetite
- poor body condition

Veterinary care is needed to deal with this condition, as it can be serious. Sometimes stool softeners will allow the animal to pass the stools more regularly; however, when the condition becomes chronic, surgery is often the only recourse.

Hazards to Your Pet

While dogs and cats are, for the most part, pretty hardy, there are certain things their digestive systems just can't handle. Of course, pets will pick up or try to eat the weirdest things, and unfortunately, many of the things we have around the house, garage, and yard can be hazardous to our pets. One acetaminophen pain-reliever tablet can be fatal for a small cat, and several slurps of antifreeze can kill a dog. Yet we use these things on a regular basis and don't think anything more about it.

Listed below are some of the things that you may have around your home:

- **Medications.** Make sure all medications are kept out of your pet's reach. Cold medications, pain relievers, dietary supplements, and herbal remedies can all be dangerous if consumed in quanity.
- **Chocolate.** This favorite food is dangerous to dogs and unfortunately, many dogs are as attracted to it as people are. All chocolate should be kept out of the reach of dogs. Cats don't have the taste buds for sweets and so are not attracted to chocolate as dogs and people are, but if a cat should eat some chocolate, it can poison the cat.
- **Insecticides.** It shouldn't surprise you that ant and roach killers, mosquito and fly sprays, and other insecticides can be poisonous to your dog or cat. But unfortunately, even flea and tick killers made for use on pets can cause a problem. Make sure you read the directions and follow the directions to the letter. Do

continues

continued

not combine killers, either, as most are designed to be used by themselves and not in combination with another chemical.

- **Rodent killers.** Rat and mouse traps and poisons can severely injure or kill your pet. Make sure traps are used out of your pet's reach, and be cautious about using any poisons. Even if your pet cannot get into the poison, a poisoned rat could stray into your pet's reach. Should your pet, dog or cat, eat even a part of the poisoned animal, your pet, too, could be poisoned.
- **Plants.** Many household and common landscaping plants can harm your pet, including azaleas, lilies, and more. Check with your local nursery or with the ASPCA Poison Control Center at *www.aspca.org/apcc* for a list of poisonous plants.

Other substances that can be a problem to pets include household cleaners, laundry cleaners, automobile cleaners and chemicals—especially antifreeze—and paints. In later chapters, I'll discuss which foods your pet should not eat, as some foods we eat are not safe for our pets.

CHAPTER TWO

The Basics of Nutrition

Nutritional science, for people as well as for animals, is a constantly changing and evolving field. Not only do the requirements for good nutrition constantly change (eggs are bad for us; no wait, they're good for us!), but we also now know that behavior is as much a part of nutrition as agricultural practices are, and that the studies of psychology and weather are also a vital part of the study of nutrition.

You might think that malnutrition would be a much simpler definition; many people feel that malnutrition and starvation are one and the same. Whereas malnutrition can be a result of starvation, there are many obese people (and dogs and cats) who also suffer from malnutrition. Malnutrition, instead, is really a deficiency of needed nutrients. A person, dog, or cat could be eating a lot of food, but if that food doesn't contain what the body needs, then malnutrition can result, usually with severe health consequences.

In this chapter, we'll take a look at the basics of nutrition: the foundation of foods, what they do in your pet's body, and how the body uses them. We'll also discuss how some of these seemingly unrelated subjects—agricultural practices and weather, for example—can affect the food we feed our pets. Although this chapter goes into quite a bit of detail regarding nutrition (perhaps more than you really wanted to know), this is important, both for your pet's health and your own. Once you understand the basics of nutrition and you know what your pet needs, you will be better equipped to make the right food choices for your dog or cat.

The Macronutrients

The macronutrients are protein, fat, and carbohydrates. These are the parts of foods that most animals need the most of for good nutrition, although the proportions vary according to the species and the individual animal eating the food.

Proteins, Amino Acids, and Enzymes

Proteins make up most of a body after water has been removed. Muscles, skin, and blood are all forms of proteins. The hair or fur, nails, and all the internal organs are made up of proteins. Proteins are also needed for healthy blood; antibodies for fighting infection are made of protein; and hormone production requires proteins. In the living body, these proteins are constantly being recycled, turned into amino acids and built again.

Proteins are made up of a variety of amino acids, but not all proteins are equal, and different proteins can have different

Plant Proteins as Fillers

Plants also contain some protein; for example, gluten meals are plant-based products that are high in plant proteins. These are often used to increase the protein levels in foods (to make the food look better), and they are considerably less expensive than animal proteins. Dogs and cats do not metabolize plant proteins nearly as well as they do animal proteins; plus, pets with cereal-grain allergies will react badly to these products. The most common allergies are to wheat, corn, and rice. In addition, wheat, corn, and rice glutens have been at the center of several recalls.

amino acids. Dogs can synthesize twelve of the twenty-two different needed amino acids; these are called nonessential because they are not required to be in the dog's diet. The other ten, called essential amino acids, must be eaten daily to prevent a protein deficiency.

The Association of American Feed Control Officials (AAFCO), the regulatory organization for animal foods, lists the following as essential amino acids for dogs:

- arginine
- histidine
- isoleucine
- leucine
- lysine

- methionine-cystine
- phenylalanine-tyrosine
- threonine
- tryptophan
- valine

Cats have thirteen essential amino acids that must be present in their diet. The one that most pet owners have heard about is taurine. That amino acid made the news a number of years ago when far too many cats were developing blindness and heart problems. Research showed that a taurine deficiency can cause both of these symptoms; commercial food manufacturers are now adding taurine to their recipes.

The AAFCO lists the following as essential amino acids for cats:

- arginine
- histidine
- isoleucine
- leucine
- lysine
- methionine-cystine
- methionine
- phenylalanine-tyrosine
- phenylalanine
- threonine
- tryptophan
- valine
- taurine

Those proteins that contain all of the essential amino acids for both dogs and cats are called complete; those that contain only some of the needed amino acids are called incomplete. (Good sources of complete proteins include eggs, muscle meats, fish, poultry, and some dairy products. Sources of incomplete proteins include beans, peas, grains, and potatoes.)

When proteins are eaten, the proteins are broken down into individual amino acids or into peptides, which are groups of amino acids. The amino acids are then absorbed into the bloodstream where they can be used for specific functions.

Proteins also contain enzymes, without which the body simply could not function. Think of enzymes as catalysts—they are involved in many different functions. Enzymes are needed for digestion, cellular repair and function, and brain function. Some enzymes work alone, while others work with coenzymes, which are usually vitamins or minerals.

A dog or cat suffering from a protein deficiency may have one or more of the following symptoms:

- chronic skin problems, including infections
- poor hair coat: dry, dull, with excessive shedding or poor pigmentation
- chronic ear problems, including infections
- hormone deficiencies, including poor or reduced adrenal gland function
- weakened immune system
- slow healing from wounds, illnesses, and injuries

Protein By-products

The quality of the protein source will affect how digestible it is, and thereby how well the body can use it. Muscle meats from beef, bison, poultry, or fish are all good sources of proteins and very digestible. By-products, however, which are listed as a protein source for many commercial dog foods, may contain good sources of protein, or they may not. The AAFCO says that chicken by-products, for example, consist of the rendered, clean parts of the carcass of a slaughtered chicken, such as necks, beaks, feet, undeveloped eggs, and intestines, and shall not contain feces or feathers except that which is inadvertently added during normal slaughtering practices.

Besides the frightening thought of feeding your dog processed feathers (or manure) under the guise of protein, the practice of using by-products makes the results of feeding a pet some commercial foods very uncertain. One batch of chicken by-products is going to be very different from another, then, because of the variety of potential ingredients. Thus the quality and nutrition will vary. Jocelynn Jacobs, DVM, says, "Pet food regulatory agencies do not allow pet food manufacturers to state the digestibility of their foods, which makes it impossible to know the quality of by-products in a meal."

The quality of protein can also vary depending upon how the animal was raised. Commercially raised beef, chickens, and turkeys have been fed growth hormones and antibiotics so they grow faster, put on meat faster, and don't become sick in overcrowded cages and pens. Farm-raised fish (as compared to wild caught fish) have been found to be sickly and full of parasites. I'll discuss the quality of foods, including proteins, in upcoming chapters.

Fats and Fatty Acids

Fats have gotten a bad rap lately. Not only are fats in foods labeled bad guys because of the increase of obesity (in people, dogs, and cats), but scientists, doctors, and the media have impressed upon us how horrible some fats can be. And, yes, too

much fat is not good for us, but fat is a nutrient that is essential to our pets' good health.

Jean Anderson, MS, and Barbara Deskins, PhD, authors of
The Nutrition Bible (William Morrow and Company, 1995) say,
"Fats are needed for the regulation of cholesterol, for the trans-
port and absorption of the fat soluble vitamins, for the function
of some hormonal processes, for healthy skin and hair, and for
energy." Fat circulates in the dog's or cat's body all the time so
that it is available when needed. Excess is stored in the body.

Three fatty acids—omega-3 fatty acid, omega-6 fatty acid,
and arachidonic acid—are considered essential fatty acids
(EFA) for dogs and cats because they are necessary for the animal to thrive. They are vital in cell structures; they help create
and maintain cell membranes. EFAs also support the immune
system, help blood movement, and much more. Omega-3 fatty
acids are found in fish (salmon, mackerel, halibut, and herring)
as well as flaxseeds and walnuts. Omega-6 fatty acids can be
found in safflower, sunflower, corn and evening primrose oils,
as well as chicken fat. Arachidonic fatty acids can be found in
fish oils.

Dogs or cats suffering from a fat or fatty acid deficiency may
have the following :

- a lack of energy for daily activities and play
- dry skin, itching, and thickened areas of skin
- a dull, dry, poor hair coat
- poor growth and slow healing from injuries or illnesses
- heart and circulatory problems, including poor blood
  clotting

Dogs and cats need a variety of fats in their diet, but too
much can lead to weight gain and obesity. Wendy Volhard and

Kerry Brown, DVM, authors of *Holistic Guide for a Healthy Dog* (Howell Book House, 2000), say, "Moderation is the key. The diet needs to have some animal fat but not too much; anything between 15 to 18 percent (of the daily calories from food) is okay." Hardworking dogs, hard-playing dogs, or dogs under stress may need more fat, though, because fat is one of the best sources of energy. Jocelynn Jacobs, DVM, says that military, police, agility, Flyball, and field-trial dogs may need 35 to 45 percent of their calories to come from fat. Herding dogs who work all day long may need 45 to 50 percent of their calories to come from fat, and sled dogs may need as much as 65 percent of their calories to come from fat.

An indoor cat who is only sporadically active, will need 10 to 15 percent of the daily calories to come from fat. An outdoor cat who is slightly more active may need a diet that is 12 to 18 percent fat. A cat under stress, either an outdoor cat in a cold climate, a cat in training (for show business or the cat-show circuit), or a cat under another type of stress, may need a diet in which 18 to 25 percent of the calories come from fat.

Carbohydrates

Carbohydrates are sugars and starches of various forms and are made up of molecules of oxygen, hydrogen, and carbon. Although carbohydrates were branded as evil by some of the diet gurus during the 1990s and early 2000s, carbs do have a place in our diets and in those of dogs. Cats have no dietary need for carbohydrates, although they can metabolize some carbs.

Carbohydrates are broken down by the body into glucose, which is then used as energy and for various bodily functions. Glucose is vital to the correct functioning of the nervous system, and dogs with low glucose levels may suffer from seizures.

The Glycemic Index: Not Just for Humans!

The speed in which the body can convert starches into sugar is what is called the glycemic index (GI). Foods with a high GI raise blood sugar levels very rapidly, providing quick bursts of energy followed by an energy letdown. Foods with a lower GI are slower to digest and therefore provide a more balanced blood sugar level.

A GI over 70 is considered high, and a GI under 55 is considered low:

- apple: 26
- barley: 25
- kidney beans: 27
- oatmeal: 49
- pasta, whole wheat: 37
- pumpkin: 75
- rice, white, short grain: 72
- yam: 51
- yogurt: 33

Keeping the blood sugar balanced and on a more even keel is much healthier for dogs and cats in many ways. When the blood sugar is stable, the dog's or cat's body is able to maintain a cellular sensitivity to insulin, which may prevent diabetes in the future. In addition, when blood sugars are stable, the dog or cat will have energy for normal activities at a more sustained rate.

On a behavioral note, dogs who eat foods with a high GI often show learning difficulties; they cannot hold still, have trouble concentrating, and have difficulty retaining what they have learned.

The body can also convert some of the glucose into glycogen, which can be stored in the liver and muscles as a quick energy reserve.

There are three groups of carbohydrates:

- Monosaccharides are simple sugars. Glucose, the sugar that carbohydrates are broken down into, is a simple sugar. Only glucose circulates in the bloodstream. Fructose, a sugar derived from fruits, is also a simple sugar.
- Disaccharides are double sugars, which means two sugars are bonded together. Sucrose is a double sugar and is the white sugar usually used in the kitchen. Lactose, maltose, and glucose are also disaccharides.
- Polysaccharides are complex carbohydrates, and they're called this because they are often made up of elaborate chains of sugar molecules. Polysaccharides, which digest much more slowly than monosaccharides or disaccharides, are found in peas, beans, grains, potatoes, and other starchy plants. These are also very good sources of vitamins, minerals, and fiber.

Some good sources of nutritious, digestible carbohydrates for pets include the following:

- alfalfa
- barley
- brown or wild rice
- flaxseed and flaxseed meal
- molasses
- oatmeal
- potatoes, including sweet potatoes and yams

The quality of the carbohydrates used in pet foods can vary for many reasons. The growing conditions, including the soil and amount of and quality of the water available can affect the nutritional value of the plants. In times of water shortages or drought, mature trees that are well established can cope. The fruit might be smaller, or the tree may drop some immature fruit, causing a smaller crop, but the tree will still produce edible fruits. Many farmers have found, though, that those fruits contain fewer carbohydrates so are less nourishing. Crops grown in depleted soils, flourishing only because of artificial fertilizers, contain equally depleted amounts of nutrients, especially minerals.

Fiber

Carbohydrates also provide fiber, which allows the intestinal tract to function well and to form stools. Although dogs and cats do not have the correct enzymes to completely digest fiber, the bacteria living in the animal's large intestine can digest the fiber if it remains in the large intestine long enough. This process is called fermentation.

For many years, fiber was called soluble or insoluble; those that could dissolve in water were called soluble. The most common sources of soluble fiber are fruits, potatoes, beans, and oatmeal. Insoluble fiber is cellulose, which forms the framework of cell walls in plants. Found in most plants, cellulose will not dissolve but does absorb water, and so it assists in stool formation and motility.

Today, however, fiber is classified by its ability to be fermented in the large intestine by the normal bacteria found there. Fiber from cellulose has a low fermentability, whereas cabbage fiber's fermentability is high. Those fibers that are easily fermented have as a side effect, though, the tendency to produce a lot of gas.

When a dog or cat eats a diet that has too many carbo-hydrates, or carbohydrates that are not easily digested, the an-imal will appear bloated, will be uncomfortable, and may have a lot of gas. Individual dogs and cats may also have sensitivi-ties toward certain foods with fiber; whereas one dog or cat may be able to ferment and pass fibers from a specific food, another dog or cat may not. That pet may appear to be un-comfortable and may have a lot of flatulence. If this happens, make note of the sources of fiber in the foods your pet has eaten, either commercial or homemade, and avoid those sources of fiber in the future.

The Micronutrients

The micronutrients are those parts of the diet that are essen-tial to good health, but are found in smaller quantities than the macronutrients. Although many of these are needed in minute amounts, they are still vital to many of the body's pro-cesses. The micronutrients includes vitamins, minerals, probi-otics, and phytonutrients.

The Vitamins

Vitamin A.   This vitamin is essential for good eyesight of both dogs and cats and is especially important for the health of the retina and for night vision. It helps keep mucus membranes healthy in both the respiratory and gastrointestinal tracts. Vita-min A also plays a part in cell reproduction, helps keep the im-mune system healthy, and is a powerful antioxidant.

Antioxidants

Antioxidants are chemicals (often vitamins) that prevent the oxidation (or breakdown) of other substances. When an apple is dipped into orange juice containing natural vitamin C, the apple will remain fresh longer without turning brown. The vitamin C in the orange juice prevents the oxidation of the apple. Oxidation is continually occurring in the body, but antioxidants grab those free radicals and prevent further damage in the body.

As a fat-soluble vitamin, excess is stored in the dog's or cat's body, primarily in the liver. It can become toxic if too much is ingested. However, when it's obtained from whole food sources, toxicity is rare.

Good sources of natural (not synthetic) vitamin A include egg yolks, fish oils, and liver.

Vitamin B Complex. There are several B vitamins, all of which are water soluble, and they are often referred to as B complex. The B vitamins are vital to many canine and feline bodily processes. They are found in many cereal grains but unfortunately are very sensitive to heat, so the process of making commercial dog and cat foods destroys most of these vitamins.

- B_1, thiamine, helps nerve cells function normally. It is important for good mental health. Dogs with a lack of vitamin B_1 often have difficulty learning.

- B_2, riboflavin, functions as a coenzyme for cell respiration. B_2 is also important for good vision and necessary for the digestion of carbohydrates.
- B_3, niacin, is needed for the digestion of proteins, fats, and carbohydrates. It also assists in blood circulation. The amino acid tryptophan can produce niacin in the body.
- B_5, pantothenic acid, is related to the functioning of the adrenal glands. It is also important for vitamin metabolism and for the conversion of other foods into energy.
- B_6, pyridoxine, helps process amino acids and is important in the development and functioning of the nervous system. A lack of this vitamin can lead to mental depression. It is also essential for red blood cell production.
- B_{12}, cyanocobalamin, is a coenzyme to a protein and works with several other amino acids. It is essential to healthy DNA and RNA and is important for good heart health and mental health. It assists in maintaining a healthy nervous system.
- Folic acid is important for the duplication of chromosomes during cell reproduction. It helps prevent birth abnormalities.

Vitamin C and Ascorbic Acid.   Vitamin C is a water-soluble vitamin that is produced by the bodies of some animals, including dogs and cats, but is not produced by humans. Since dogs and cats can create vitamin C themselves, there is no listed requirement for it. However, many experts do believe that animals often do not produce enough, especially in times of stress.

Although ascorbic acid is often referred to as vitamin C (and vice versa) that is not technically correct. Ascorbic acid is the antioxidant portion of vitamin C, not the complete vitamin.

Vitamin C has many uses, including that of an antioxidant. It works to prevent bruising, fights infections, is vital for the production of cartilage, and is known to slow down the development of cataracts. It helps to stabilize blood sugar, to prevent gum disease, and much more.

Although there are no recommended dosages for vitamin C for dogs and cats, it is relatively safe. Excess is excreted through the urine, although high dosages can cause diarrhea. Very high dosages given over time have been known to interfere with the absorption of calcium.

Vitamin C is available in fruits, especially citrus fruits, and also in some vegetables.

Vitamin D.   This vitamin is important for the correct absorption of calcium and phosphorus and, as such, is necessary for the formation and maintenance of healthy bones and teeth. It also aids the immune system, works with the circulatory system, and is important for correct thyroid function.

Vitamin D is fat soluble, which means fat is required in the diet for it to be absorbed. It can also be produced in small amounts when dogs and cats are exposed to sunlight. This amount, however, is not enough; dietary vitamin D is needed too. Dietary supplements are discussed in more detail in chapter 6.

Although vitamin D is a relatively safe vitamin, it can become toxic if large dosages (more than 10,000 international units per kilogram of food) are given over a period of time, because excess fat-soluble vitamins are retained by the body. If the vitamin D is fed to the dog through whole food sources, though, such as egg yolks, toxicity is not a problem.

Vitamin E.   This is another fat-soluble vitamin that is essential to good canine and feline health. Vitamin E is necessary for nerves and muscles to function properly, and it is a power-ful antioxidant, perhaps one of the most potent. This vitamin has also been claimed to promote good mental health, reduce the risk of heart disease, promote normal blood clotting, and help maintain healthy skin and hair.

Vitamin E is a very safe vitamin, and toxicity is rarely a problem, especially if gained from whole food sources. In addition, the natural forms of vitamin E, such as those from eggs, liver, green foods, and rose hips, have been found to be more effective than the synthetic formulations.

Vitamin K.   Vitamin K is a relatively unknown vitamin; this isn't one that is commonly heard of or talked about. However, this fat-soluble vitamin can play an important part in your pet's continued good health. Vitamin K is needed for correct calcium absorption and, as a result, for healthy bones and teeth and correct blood clotting.

Vitamin K can be produced in the body from natural food sources, so there is no recommended dosage for dogs and cats (or for people, for that matter). However, deficiencies in vita-min K will show up as bleeding disorders from poor clotting factors in the blood.

Natural sources of vitamin K include dark green vegetables such as kale, spinach, and broccoli. Synthetic vitamin K is usually not recommended, as incidences of toxicity have been reported.

The Minerals

Calcium.   This is a vitally important mineral; without it, there would be no life. The vast majority of calcium in the body is in the bones, but it is also important for muscle con-traction and relaxation, for nerve transmissions, for healthy blood, and for correct hormone levels. Calcium also works as a coenzyme for many chemical processes in the body.

Dietary calcium can be found in dairy products and vegeta-bles. Supplemental calcium is found in a number of different formulations, including calcium lactate, which is converted into calcium bicarbonate, which is easily absorbed by the body.

A calcium deficiency can result in rickets or thyroid dys-function; an excess can cause skeletal disorders and other mineral deficiencies.

Phosphorus. This mineral works with calcium and many ex-perts refer to the two minerals as one pair, calcium-phosphorus, as they cannot function without the other. The proportions of calcium and phosphorus are very important, as too much cal-cium can result in skeletal disorders and growth problems. The ideal is 1.3 parts calcium to 1 part phosphorus. This mineral can be found in meats, including beef, fish, and poultry.

A phosphorus deficiency can cause rickets and thyroid dys-function; an excess can cause a calcium deficieny.

Copper. This essential mineral works with iron in the body; it is also vital to the production of hemoglobin and red blood cells. Excess vitamin C may impair the body's ability to absorb copper. Excess copper is stored in the liver; if the copper accu-mulates or the body cannot use the supply in the liver, copper toxicity may result. Dogs and cats can metabolize copper from beef, chicken, and other animal liver, and from water that flows through copper pipes.

A copper deficiency can cause anemia and poor bone development, as excess in the liver can cause copper toxicity.

Iodine.　Iodine is important for proper thyroid function, and the thyroid hormones are important for cellular metabolism. Iodine can be found in fish, liver, and kelp.

A deficiency can cause growth and development problems, as well as reproductive problems; an excess can cause goiter.

Iron.　The formation of hemoglobin depends on iron; in fact, iron combined with oxygen gives blood its bright red color. Iron is also important to the muscles, as it is needed for the formation of myoglobin, which supplies oxygen to the muscles. Iron absorption requires protein and vitamin C. Iron can be found in meats, vegetables, and whole grains.

A deficiency can cause anemia; an excess is very rare because only as much as is needed is absorbed.

Magnesium.　This mineral is found in the bones. It is also found in the cells, where it works with enzymes to metabolize carbohydrates. It is also important in the electrical processes of nerves and muscles. It is found in dairy products, whole grains, and vegetables.

A deficiency can cause bone deformities; an excess is unlikely, as the body determines how much is to be absorbed.

Manganese.　This mineral activates many enzymes and aids in the development of bones and connective tissues. It works with enzymes and assists in maintaining glucose levels. It is found in whole grains and vegetables.

A deficiency can cause skeletal and growth problems; an excess is rare.

Selenium.   Selenium is an antioxidant that works with fatty acids in the system. It supports the immune system, works with the reproductive system, and is thought to help protect against cancer. It is found in fish, meat, and whole grains, although the cooking of foods reduces its effectiveness.

A deficiency can cause cardiac and skeletal abnormalities; an excess can cause heart, liver, or kidney problems.

Zinc.   This often-forgotten mineral is very important. It is essential for the metabolism of foods and is a coenzyme for more than twenty-five different enzymes involved with digestion. It is a component of insulin, aids in the healing of wounds, and supports the immune system. Zinc can be found in meats and egg yolks.

A deficiency can cause skin problems, hair pigmentation problems, and poor growth. An excess causes calcium and copper deficiencies.

More Essential Nutrients Your Pet Should Have

The classification of micronutrients originally contained just vitamins and minerals, but today nutritionists and those studying the field of nutrition, for people and animals, have agreed there are several other things that need to be included in this classification.

Probiotics

The large intestine, when healthy, contains a flourishing colony of bacteria. These small organisms initially may seem to be disgusting, but they are important for the animal's health.

Not only do they complete the sequence of digestion, but they also keep dangerous bacteria at bay.

These beneficial bacteria colonies can be disturbed by illnesses and a poor diet, and can be wiped out by long-term antibiotic use. Other medications, especially steroids, can also affect the bacteria populations.

Probiotics are supplements that can boost the beneficial bacteria colonies in the large intestine. Yogurt that contains live, active cultures (it will say so on the label) is an excellent probiotic, as are acidophilus supplements.

The high heats of commercial dog-food preparation will kill any probiotics present in the food; these need to be added to the diet when the food is served.

Phytonutrients

Phytonutrients, sometimes called phytochemicals, are not vitamins or minerals, but they are still potentially important foods. These are parts of plants that have been shown to have beneficial properties. Some, like the capsaicin in chili peppers, have well-known, proven abilities. (Capasaicin is both a pain reliever and a cancer fighter.) Others, like the genistein in soybeans, are still being researched. (It is thought to reduce the risk of breast and mammary gland cancers.)

As more research is done on these chemicals, the foods they come from are still good, nutritious foods, and the benefits come with the foods. For dogs and cats, the foods include berries, dark green vegetables, tomatoes, carrots, and yams.

Although much research still needs to be done on many phytonutrients, we do know that the high heat of commercial dog-food processing kills many plant nutrients.

Water

Water is one of the most often forgotten essentials for life. Sure, we drink water when thirsty, and we refill our dogs' and cats' bowls, but we don't think about how vital water is to life.

All of the body's functions depend on water. Water is necessary for respiration, for digestion, for assimilation and absorption of nutrients, for the metabolism of nutrients, for temperature regulation, and for waste removal.

Jocelynn Jacobs, DVM, says, "Dogs can tolerate a dietary deficiency in protein, fats, vitamins, or minerals for a short time. However, dehydration will lead to a diminished performance quickly, and in severe cases, can even lead to death."

It is almost impossible to figure out exactly how much water any one dog or cat might need on a daily basis. The needs will vary according to the animal's size and weight, health, activity levels, what the animal is eating, and even the weather. Given all these factors, it's best to make sure that your pet always has clean drinking water available. If your dog is participating in a sport or is working, water should be offered as often as possible. During travel, water should be offered whenever your dog or cat appears warm (he or she is panting, looking for shade, or appears uncomfortable) and during travel stops.

CHAPTER THREE

The Big Debate over Commercial Pet Foods

You probably have your own feelings about commercial pet foods; most pet owners do. But if you want to incite a riot, go to a gathering of serious pet owners (perhaps a dog or cat show) and start a conversation about commercial pet foods! There will be some people claiming commercial pet foods are the work of the devil, invented to torture and kill our pets at a young age by causing cancer and other horrible diseases. A few other owners will question that opinion and will show off their healthy pets as an example of the quality of those very same foods.

This debate has been ongoing for many years; when I first researched pet foods in the early 1990s, people were already questioning the quality of commercial pet foods. The recalls of the late 1990s and early 2000s, and most especially the huge recall of 2007, really escalated the debates. But before we take a look at those foods, let's talk first about what canines and felines ate before the introduction of commercial foods.

Food in the Wild

Let's take a look at the wild canines we see on television all the time: wolves. Animal shows showing predators always show wolves chasing a deer or caribou. While wolves do hunt large prey animals, these large animals are not their only source of food, because hunting large animals carries some risk to the wolf. Hunting large game can use up a lot of energy: chasing it, separating it from its brethren, and then taking it down. A large prey animal can also fight hard and potentially hurt the wolf (or wolves). A hurt predator cannot hunt and may go hungry; plus, if the wolf is injured badly enough, it could die. And not all hunts are successful; sometimes the prey animal gets away, and all that energy used for hunting is wasted.

What we don't always see on television is that wild canines are opportunistic; they will eat just about anything they can find, including fallen fruits and buried plant tubers. In addition, although wolves often prefer large prey, they will also eat mice and other small animals. Many researchers studying wolves in Alaska and northern Canada were actually surprised at the numbers of small animals the wolves ate.

About twenty years ago, I watched a pack of feral dogs that lived in the hills outside of Palmdale, California. These dogs were strays and abandoned dogs, the ones who were strong enough, wily enough, or lucky enough to survive their initial abandonment. There were a variety of breeds and mixes, from a miniature poodle to a German shepherd. The poodle, actually, was one of the leaders; she was small, but she was smart and tough. These dogs ate anything they could catch or find, from garbage in garbage cans to rabbits and gophers to fallen fruits. They were very opportunistic. I watched these dogs off and on for about two years; although their mortality rate was high because of accidents, parasites, collisions with cars, and cold winters, very few of the dogs who worked with the pack went hungry for long, primarily because they were willing to eat anything.

Wild or feral felines, however, are not nearly as willing to eat anything they come across as canines are. Almost all cats prefer a fresh, clean kill (ideally one of their own). Cats will rarely scavenge, and most will avoid garbage. Cats don't like fallen fruits, will not dig up tubers, and often won't even eat from one of their own previous kills if the meat has begun to decay.

Dogs and cats also vary in what they eat of their kill. Both eat muscle meats and the internal organs. Dogs, however, often eat the gastrointestinal tract, thereby gaining some nutrition from the foods the prey animal ate. Many cats, however, set the intestinal tract aside, ignoring it.

How Domestication Has Changed Diets

The theories abound as to how and why dogs and cats were domesticated and whether people initiated the process or the animals did. But once dogs and cats joined with people, they began to eat what the people ate. They had leftover meats, organs, skin, and bones, and the dogs also shared leftover agricultural products including fruits, grains, nuts, and vegetables. The relationship was symbiotic; the dogs, cats, and people benefited.

This relationship continued for thousands of years and on into modern times. My paternal grandparents farmed in the Midwest up until my grandfather passed away. They always had dogs and cats that helped around the farm, and they were fed anything that the family might also eat. When milking the cows, my grandfather would give both the dogs and cats some of the milk. The dogs and cats also got eggs from the chickens and geese, and when an animal was butchered for meat, they got that, too. And of course, both dogs and cats got leftovers from the table.

The Birth of Commercial Pet Foods

The first commercial dog food was created in England in the 1860s. James Spratt, an American salesman, was visiting England, where he saw street dogs lined up along a wharf waiting for sailors to toss out hardtack biscuits and leftover (usually rotten) foods. Spratt, a dog lover himself, decided he could come up with a better product and created a bone-shaped biscuit made from wheat, vegetables, beet roots, and beef blood. It was introduced to the American dog-owning public in 1890.

In 1907, F. H. Bennett created Milk-Bone dog foods and biscuits as direct competition to Spratt's products, and these two dominated the market until Ken-L Ration created the first canned dog food in the 1920s.

After World War I, when cars and tractors began replacing horses and mules, canned dog food containing these meats quickly gained popularity. However, canned foods were looked upon with less favor as the United States became involved in World War II and tin became too expensive. In addition, the surplus of horses disappeared during this era. Purina, a maker of feeds for farm animals, began flooding the markets with dry, kibbled dog foods in 1957; cat foods followed in 1962.

Most of these early foods were introduced with little research behind them. They were made from ingredients that were readily available (such as wheat and the surplus horses and mules) and were relatively inexpensive. But eventually research did become a part of the industry.

In 1906 Burton Hill founded Hill's Packing Company. In 1948, Mark Morris Sr., DVM, met with Hill to discuss a partnership so that Hill's Packing Company could package Morris's first veterinary dog-food formulas, the first of which was for dogs with kidney disease. In 1968, Mark Morris Jr., DVM, followed in his father's footsteps when he created Science Diet foods.

Pet Foods as Time-savers

Commercial pet foods were introduced to the public as time-savers; they were convenient. During World War II, especially, when large numbers of women worked jobs away from the home for the first time, convenience foods for both people and their pets became important. The first so-called TV dinners were introduced in the 1940s, and they, too, were marketed as convenient for the family.

These commercial foods were also labeled as balanced and complete and much better for the family dog than scraps from the table. Sales representatives convinced veterinarians that these foods were more nutritious and, hence, healthier for their customers' pets. In addition, veterinarians began selling the foods in their clinics and so had a monetary incentive to promote the foods.

The field of advertising and marketing has also grown up on commercial pet foods. By utilizing the bond people have with their pets, the advertising people created print ads first, for newspapers and magazines, and sold the pet-owning public on the idea of these convenient pet foods. A photo of a dog and owner looking deeply into each other's eyes as the headline said, FEED SUCH-AND-SUCH DOG FOOD FOR THE LIFE OF YOUR DOG! Thinking that this food would extend the dog's life and that the dog would be forever grateful, people bought the food.

Advertising dog and cat foods really came into its own with the advent of television. Often we see commercials showing healthy dogs cavorting in green fields, or happily purring cats lapping up canned cat foods from a delicate bowl. And just as often, reading the ingredients of those foods is a lesson in truth—or the lack thereof—in advertising.

Problems with Pet Foods Today

One would think that with all the research that pet food companies say they do, dogs and cats would be significantly healthier today than in years past and live for many years longer. Unfortunately that's not true.

In the 1970s, pet health declined considerably. Cancer, allergies, and arthritis became much more prevalent, as did kidney and liver disease. Many veterinarians, especially those who prefer a more holistic approach to veterinary medicine, believe that commercial pet foods are a big part of today's pet-health problem. As mentioned in chapter 2, the high heats needed to process pet foods can kill many of the nutrients. The B complex vitamins, which are essential to so many bodily processes, are killed by heat; so too are probiotics, phytonutrients, and many enzymes. Although many pet-food makers try to add

Antibiotics in Livestock

Seventy percent of all the antibiotics sold in the United States today are used on farms and are fed or injected into the livestock that will be sold either as human food or as pet food. Chickens, turkeys, pigs, sheep, dairy cattle, and beef cattle are all given these antibiotics, because in the 1950s, studies showed that livestock given these antibiotics gained weight faster.

Mary C. Pearl said in her 2007 *Discover* magazine column, "Better Planet," that other factors, such as improved breeding practices, better farm management, and newer feed formulations, also spurred the improved growth, but those factors were not taken into account for those studies.

Today, however, all this antibiotic use has created a surge of bacteria that is now resistant to many antibiotics. This affects not only the livestock and the people who work with the livestock, but also those who eat the meat and anyone who comes into contact with the resistant bacteria. Recent studies have shown that penicillin resistance has grown by 300 percent in recent years, and cefotaxime resistance has grown by more than 1,000 percent.

these ingredients to the food after processing, most of these efforts involve synthetic forms, and studies in the past decade have shown that synthetic vitamins, minerals, and other nutrients are usually not as digestible, as easily metabolized, and often not nearly as effective as the natural ingredient.

In addition, pet foods today contain many foods that dogs and cats would not normally eat. Neither dogs nor cats were designed to eat wheat, corn, rice, or other cereal grains, yet these are the mainstay ingredients for hundreds of commercial foods. Because it's cheap, soy in its many forms (soy flour, soybean meal, and soy grits) is found in many pet foods, even though many pets have bad reactions to it (bloating and gas).

The quality of the ingredients in the commercial food also affects the health of the pet who eats it. The grains and other carbohydrates may be left over from processing human foods, or may be tainted foods not allowed in human food processing, or may have been grown in depleted soils. The meats may be leftovers and by-products, or worse. The food can be full of additives, preservatives, and artificial colors and flavorings. But there is some good news; not all pet foods are horrible. Below we'll talk more about food quality.

Commercial Foods Vary in Quality

Just as foods for people vary in quality, so, too, do pet foods. And again, just as with food for people, the better nutrition comes with the foods made with better ingredients and processed in such a way that the nutrients are not destroyed. There are many different kinds of pet foods, many different quality levels, and a variety of forms of food. Let's take a quick look first at some classifications of pet foods:

- **Generic and grocery-store foods**. These foods are designed to be sold at a low price so that many people will buy them. They are usually made from the cheapest of ingredients, which usually includes cereal grains such as corn and wheat. The animal protein often comes from by-products or by-product meals. Artificial colors, flavors, and preservatives are common in these foods. In addition, the vitamins and minerals are often synthetic rather than from whole foods. Although thousands of pets can eat these foods without problems, many others will develop allergies or nutritional deficiencies.

- **Premium foods.** These foods are generally not found in grocery stores but instead will be sold at pet stores or at veterinary hospitals. Although the price is higher, the quality is usually better too. However, there is a wide range of quality within this classification, and some of these foods may still have questionable ingredients as well as synthetic vitamins and minerals.

- **Super-premium foods.** These are usually the most expensive foods. They are usually made from the best ingredients, but there can be a wide variation in formulas and recipes, some leaning toward more natural ingredients and others using more artificial additives.

- **Natural foods.** Of the commercial pet foods, these are the foods usually recommended by holistic veterinarians and those who study nutrition. The foods considered natural are supposed to contain nothing artificial; no artificial colors, flavorings, or preservatives, and no synthetic vitamins or minerals. They usually use human-grade ingredients and whole foods rather than just processed parts of the foods.

- **Organic.** The U.S. Department of Agriculture says, "Pet food regulations are a better fit under the livestock section of the organic rules. Ingredients and additives permitted in pet food are regulated similarly to livestock feed."

A Study in Contrasts: Two Dog Foods

AN EXCELLENT FOOD

The Honest Kitchen produces dehydrated natural pet foods in a plant that makes foods for people, and the ingredients are all human grade. Embark, a grain-free, low-carb dog food, lists the following ingredients: hormone-free USDA turkey, organic flaxseed, potatoes, celery, spinach, carrots, coconut, apples, organic kelp, eggs, sesame seeds, bananas, cranberries, and rosemary. Protein is 29 percent; carbohydrates are 35 percent; fat is 16 percent; fiber is 9 percent; moisture is 8 percent.

A NOT-SO-EXCELLENT FOOD

A commercial dry dog food you'll find at some feed stores and dollar stores, lists these ingredients: ground yellow corn, wheat middlings, corn gluten feed, rice bran, meat and bonemeal, soybean meal, animal fat preserved with BHA, and a long list of mostly synthetic vitamins and minerals. The protein is no less than 18 percent; fat is no less than 7 percent; fiber is no more than 9 percent; and moisture is no more than 12 percent.

EXPLANATION

The second food is extremely low in protein, especially animal protein, and extremely high in cereal-grain carbohydrates. There is no muscle meat in the recipe, and since the meat in the recipe is listed as "meat and bonemeal" you don't even know what species of meat-producing animals are in the food. The first food, in comparison, sounds like it would be good enough for us to eat!

In addition, a food must be made with a minimum of 70 percent organic ingredients to be labeled "made with organic" and at least 95 percent organic to be labeled "organic."

However, even with these classifications, it is difficult to determine the quality of a food unless you understand how to read the pet food label, so let's take a look at labels.

Deciphering Pet-Food Labels

The importance of understanding pet-food labels cannot be overemphasized. The adage says, "We are what we eat," and the same applies to our pets. If our dogs and cats eat junk food with cheap or inappropriate ingredients, then they will eventually suffer for it.

The Regulation of Labels

The makers of pet foods cannot label dog and cat foods as they wish; they are required to follow a number of different regulations as to what must be on the label. Whereas this can help the consumer as certain information is required to be on the label, it can also hurt the consumer as other information is not allowed on the label. This quagmire has been created by a number of different agencies.

- **The Food and Drug Administration (FDA)** has a division called the **Center for Veterinary Medicine (CVM).** The CVM specifies which ingredients are allowed in foods, which manufacturing processes are allowed, and they set the standards for health claims for the foods. For example, if a manufacturer says a food will prevent or help treat a specific condition, such as kidney disease, that claim must be substantiated through the FDA first. Unfortunately, the FDA only inspects about 1 percent of the imported foods it is supposed to regulate; and its numbers of inspectors is down significantly.

- **The Association of American Feed Control Officials (AAFCO)** is a nongovernmental, nonregulatory organization. The AAFCO comprises experts in their fields, usually state feed control officials, and members of the FDA and USDA. The AAFCO sets the standards for minimum and maximum amounts of certain nutrients in foods. The AAFCO also makes recommendations regarding pet-food labels, including the format so that information is presented in an organized manner.
- **The United States Department of Agriculture (USDA)** is the governmental arm that oversees pet foods and their labels. The USDA states what can and cannot be present on the labels.
- **The National Research Council (NRC)** evaluates research that has been done on pet foods and pet nutrition, and after evaluating this research, it makes recommendations for pet foods.
- **The Pet Food Institute (PFI)** is an organization that represents pet food manufacturers. Primarily a lobbying group, the PFI promotes pet-food issues with the government or, as it did during the pet-food recalls, defends the pet food manufacturers to the government.

In addition, the individual states (usually the agricultural departments) are also involved. Dave Syverson, chair of the AAFCO Pet Food Committee, says in his article "Questions and Answers Concerning Pet Food Regulations" on the AAFCO Web site (www.aafco.org), "Most of the routine day to day regulation is performed by the states, however, there is a necessary synergy between the state feed control officials and the U.S. Food and Drug Administration." Some states have become very involved in the pet foods manufactured within their state jurisdictions, while others are not. Once the foods have been manufactured (within an individual state, or as we saw in the 2007 recalls, even in another country), the transportation of those foods is governed by the FDA.

With so many organizations involved, it's easy to see why pet-food labels, and the industry as a whole, can be so confusing. It's also easy to see why so little gets done; after all, who is really in charge?

Required Elements

The first required element on the food package is the product name. This is how you recognize the food and usually the first thing you look for on a package. This may be as simple as "Fido's Lamb and Rice Kibble," or it may be a more elaborate name designed to attract your attention, such as "Fido's First Choice All Natural Lamb and Brown Rice for Puppies." We'll discuss the terms *natural* and *for life stages* later, but right now just realize the food's name is designed to get your attention and to hopefully help you remember that food so you buy it again later.

The package must also have the manufacturer's name and a means of contact, either by address, telephone number, or Web site. The label must also state that it is dog food, so that it won't be confused with cat food or food for people. The package will also have the net weight of the food inside the package.

A Study in Contrasts: Two Cat Foods

AN EXCELLENT FOOD

The pet-food company Old Mother Hubbard makes some very good commercial pet foods. Their new dry cat food, Wellness CORE, is receiving rave reviews. The formula is grain free and contains lots of nutrient-rich meats. The ingredients list begins with deboned turkey, deboned chicken, chicken meal, whitefish meal, potatoes, salmon meal, natural chicken flavor, chicken fat preserved with tocopherols, tomato pumice, cranberries, chicory root extract, salmon oil, and flaxseeds. Protein is not less than 50 percent; fat is not less than 18 percent; fiber is not more than 3 percent; and moisture is not more than 11 percent.

A NOT-SO-EXCELLENT FOOD

A typical commercial dry cat food may begin its list of ingredients with ground yellow corn, corn gluten meal, chicken by-product meal, meat and bonemeal, animal fat preserved with tocopherols, corn germ meal, soybean meal, turket by-product meal, brewer's dried yeast, and mostly synthetic vitamins and minerals, artificial colors, flavorings, and preservatives.

EXPLANATION

The second food is a cereal-based food with some meat by-products and meals. By-products may be made of many different parts of the animal, and the digestibility will vary from batch to batch. In addition, natural forms of vitamins and minerals, especially those from whole foods, are more easily dissolved than the synthetic ones.

The package must also have a nutritional adequacy state-ment. Before a pet food can be labeled complete and bal-anced, it must adhere to the AAFCO guidelines to that effect. To do this, the food must be tested in feeding trials or show that it has been formulated according to AAFCO's nutritional guidelines. The debates are ongoing as to which is better.

Some experts feel that feeding trials are the best method of proving a food because dogs or cats have to eat this food for a period of time. Other experts state that the feeding trials are too short (often as short as six months) and involve too few dogs or cats (as few as eight). In any case, while the debates continue, the food will have to state which method was used.

If the food was made for a specific purpose, such as for pup-pies or kittens, for senior dogs or cats, or for a medical purpose, it will also have to show that on the label. The AAFCO has established two dog- or cat-food nutrient profiles: one for growth or lactation and one for adult maintenance. Foods la-beled for these feeding groups must adhere to these standards. There is presently no standard for older dogs or cats, nor is there a standard for active dogs.

The Guaranteed Analysis

The guaranteed analysis provides the percentages of several parts of the food. The analysis will list the minimum percent-age of protein in the food, the minimum percentage of fat, the maximum percentage of crude fiber, and the maximum per-centage of moisture.

These percentages are of the food as it is packaged, so the differences between a kibble food that is low in moisture can-not be directly compared to a canned food with a lot of water. Foods should be compared by dry-matter basis. See sidebar.

The Accuracy of Nutritional Claims

Should we be concerned about the fact that the studies being conducted as to the nutritional benefits of pet foods are being done by the pet-food makers themselves? These companies have an obvious commercial interest in these foods. Wouldn't it be smarter to have an unrelated business or organization do the studies?

The editors of *Scientific American* magazine, in the September 2007 issue, asked this same question in regard to foods for people. They stated in the opinion column, "Unfortunately, food industry money seems to distort nutritional studies." They continued by saying that studies supported by food companies were more likely to favor their sponsors than those studies funded by disinterested parties.

It stands to reason that the same would apply to our pets' foods. Perhaps there should be more studies conducted by someone other than the commercial food companies themselves.

The *guaranteed analysis* is what it says: a guarantee that there is so much protein, fat, fiber, and water in the food, but it does not state anything about the *quality* of the food. Nor does it say anything about the digestibility of the food. A package might list protein at 20 percent, but it will not break it down into how much is animal protein or vegetable protein. You have to look at this listing and then look at the ingredients to try and determine what is being used to produce those percentages.

Did you also notice that there is no listing for carbohydrates? Although many pet owners want to know what the percentage of carbohydrates is, those are usually not listed. You can, however, check the dog or cat food manufacturer's Web site, where the carbohydrates are often listed, or you can call the manufacturer and ask for the percentage of carbohydrates.

Dry-Matter Basis

When comparing foods of different types—such as canned and dry kibble or dry kibble and raw frozen—it's important to compare like to like. Therefore, the foods should be compared on a dry-matter basis. Linda Bren, author of "Pet Food: The Lowdown on Labels" from the May/June 2001 *FDA Consumer* newsletter, says, "Canned foods typically contain about 75 percent water, while dry foods contain only about 10 percent."

Look on the label of one of the foods you have at home. See the percentage for moisture? Subtract that from 100 percent. What is remaining is the percentage of dry matter. To find the dry matter percentage of another nutrient, such as fat, divide the percentage of fat by the percentage of dry matter.

For example, a commercial dry cat food lists moisture as 12 percent. That subtracted from 100 gives me 88 as the percentage of dry matter within the food. However, a canned cat food lists moisture as 75 percent. That subtracted from 100 gives me 25 percent dry matter.

When you do this to several foods, you can then compare them on a like basis and get a better idea of what each food will provide to your pet.

The Listing of Ingredients

The FDA requires that pet foods be nutritious and that they contain no harmful substances. The term that is often used is *generally recognized as safe (GRAS)*. Note that it does not say, "This is safe." The Federal Food, Drug and Cosmetic Act, sections 201(s) and 409, states, "Any substance that is intentionally added to a food is a food additive, and is subject to premarket review and approval by the FDA, unless the substance is generally recognized, among qualified experts, as having been adequately shown to be safe under conditions for its intended use." And the definition continues. Unfortunately, there are so many criteria and exclusions for GRAS— so many loopholes—that many things can slip through, intentionally or unintentionally.

The foods are listed on the label in decreasing order by weight (not amount). Therefore, a meat, which might contain 70 percent water, is going to be heavier than another ingredient, such as wheat, which may only have 12 percent water, even though there could potentially be far more wheat in the food than meat.

Manufacturers can follow the rules pertaining to listing ingredients yet, in doing so, may still trick the consumer. If a food label lists beef, wheat germ, wheat flour, wheat middlings, and so on, you might be tempted to think that because it's listed first, this would be a beef-based food. In reality, though, with the second, third, and fourth ingredients all wheat, there is far more wheat than beef. Jocelynn Jacobs, DVM, author of *Performance Dog Nutrition* (Sno Shire Publications, 2005), calls this the split-ingredient trick and says that it's done because "most dog and cat food companies know that we want to see a meat protein source listed first on the label."

Some Sample Pet-Food Definitions

Many pet owners do not understand what some of the terms used on dog- and cat-food labels mean, especially in regard to ingredients. Here are some of the ingredients commonly used in pet foods and their definitions. Many of these definitions have been abbreviated. Go to the AAFCO Web site at www.aafco.org for the entire list of ingredients and for the full definitions. Beware, though, these definitions can change and often the list is revised yearly. (*Information in italics is this writer's comment or explanation.*)

MEATS AND ANIMAL PROTEINS

- **Animal digest:** Material that results from chemical and/or enzymatic hydrolysis of clean and undecomposed animal tissue. (*The animal used is not stated.*) The animal tissues used shall be exclusive of hair, horns, hooves and feathers, except in such trace amounts as might unavoidably occur in good factory practices. (*In other words, the animal tissues are broken down, either through a chemical process or by boiling in water, and the resulting soup becomes a part of the pet food. Note that "trace amounts" of the undesirable ingredients is not defined.*)
- **Chicken by-product meal:** Consists of the ground, rendered (*fat and water removed*) clean parts of the carcass of slaughtered chickens, such as necks, feet, undeveloped eggs, and intestines. The animal tissues used shall be exclusive of hair, horns, hooves, and

continues

continued

feathers, except in such trace amounts as might unavoidably occur in good factory practices. *(Note again: "Trace amounts" is not defined. By-products, whether they are chicken, beef, or any other meat-producing animal, are a variable ingredient, as amounts of specific parts will change according to the batch being processed.)*

- **Lamb meal:** Rendered *(fat and water removed)* tissue from young sheep, without added blood, hair, hooves, horns, skin, manure, or stomach contents, except in such trace amounts as might unavoidably occur in good factory processes. *(Again, "trace amounts" is not defined.)*

- **Meat:** The clean flesh from slaughtered animals; limited to the skeletal flesh and/or the tongue, diaphragm, heart or esophagus, without fat, sinew, skin, nerve, or blood vessels. *(Meat from a specific species will be labeled as such: "turkey," for example. If meat is from a variety of sources, especially mixed sources—rabbits, goats, pigs, sheep, etc.—it will be labeled simply "meat.")*

FATS

- **Animal fat:** Obtained from the tissues of mammals and/or poultry in the commercial processes of rendering or extracting. *(What mammals or poultry are used is not stated.)*
- **Beef tallow:** Fat from cattle.
- **Oil:** Liquid fat extracted from plant sources.

continues

CARBOHYDRATES

- **Barley:** Consists of at least 80 percent barley and must not contain more than 3 percent heat-damaged kernels, 6 percent foreign material, 20 percent other grains or 10 percent wild oats. *(Take a look at the numbers: Barley can contain up to 20 percent of other grains. One grain out of five could be other than barley. This is a lot if your pet is allergic to some cereal grains.)*
- **Beet pulp:** Consists of the dried residue from sugar beets, which has been cleaned and extracted in the process of making sugar. *(This is a very controversial ingredient. Manufacturers use it because they say it's a good source of fiber. Many pet-food experts claim it is a common cause of allergies, slows digestion too much, and still contains too much sugar.)*
- **Peanut hulls:** This is the outer shell of the peanut. *(It is a by-product that is added as a fiber source to make the pet feel full. It can be a source of mold contamination that can make pets very ill.)*
- **Ground corn:** The entire ear of corn ground, without husks, with no greater portion of cob than occurs in the ear corn in its natural state. *(This is not just the corn kernel that you might eat; it is the kernel and the cob ground together.)*

Additives

Most pet-food manufacturers include a number of different additives in the pet-food recipes. Those might include artificial sweeteners (dogs have taste buds for sweet things, although cats do not), spices, flavor enhancers, drying agents, anticaking agents, and much, much more.

Preservatives are added to commercial pet foods to retard the spoilage of the food. Without preservatives the fats in the foods would become rancid; this destroys the nutrients in the foods and creates toxins that would poison your pet. Chemical preservatives, especially ethoxyquin, BHA, BHT, and sodium metabisulphite, have been listed as generally regarded as safe for use in pet foods, but they are also known to cause problems.

- **Butylated hydroxyanisole (BHA):** BHA is known to have caused allergic reactions in pets; it can also cause liver and kidney problems.
- **Butylated hydroxytoluene (BHT):** BHT can cause liver and kidney problems.
- **Sodium metabisulphite:** This chemical preservative has been linked to problems in people, including weakness, loss of consciousness, and brain damage.
- **Ethoxyquin:** This preservative has also been used as a pesticide, insecticide, and a hardening agent for the process of making rubber.

Shawn Messonnier, DVM, the author of *Natural Health Bible for Dogs & Cats* (Prima Publishing, 2001) and a practicing holistic veterinarian in Plano, Texas, says, "Certainly no one would argue that we have received many benefits from chemicals. However, whenever possible, it would be in the pet's best interest if non-chemical alternatives (natural antioxidants and preservatives) were used."

Other Things on the Label (or Not)

If you read closely, you may see some other things on the label that could be important to you. Unfortunately, there

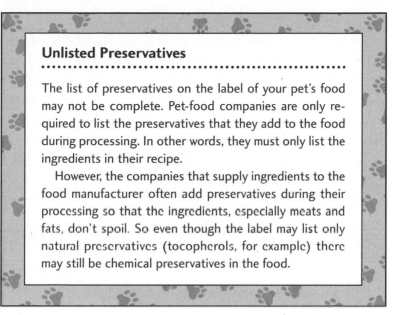

Unlisted Preservatives

The list of preservatives on the label of your pet's food may not be complete. Pet-food companies are only required to list the preservatives that they add to the food during processing. In other words, they must only list the ingredients in their recipe.

However, the companies that supply ingredients to the food manufacturer often add preservatives during their processing so that the ingredients, especially meats and fats, don't spoil. So even though the label may list only natural preservatives (tocopherols, for example) there may still be chemical preservatives in the food.

are other things that are not on the label that you should know.

Are you looking for a more natural pet food? The AAFCO has stated that the word *natural* cannot be used on a pet-food label if any of the ingredients are chemically synthesized. However, if the vitamins and minerals are chemically synthesized, the label can read, "Natural, with added vitamins and minerals."

Many pet owners are very concerned about preservatives in the food their pet eats. Most holistic veterinarians believe that most of the chemical preservatives, including the hotly debated ethoxyquin (see page 60), are not good for dogs or cats. This has caused many manufacturers to turn to tocopherols. Tocopherols are a mixture of vitamins C, E, and citric acid. They have a shorter shelf life than the chemical preservatives but are generally recognized as healthier for our pets.

One of the things you often will not see on the label is a small or subtle change in the pet-food recipe. Many pet-food manufacturers will use what is called a variable formulation. They will slightly change the food's recipe from batch to batch, depending upon the availability or price of the ingredients. You may find your dog or cat does well on one batch of the food yet has trouble on the next batch.

Dr. Jacobs says, "The AAFCO does not allow the dog food manufacturers to list the quality of their ingredients on their labels." The pet-food makers can use this to their advantage, using lesser-quality cuts of meats or poorer-quality ingredients to make the food. The food's digestibility suffers, yet the ingredients on the label still appear to be good.

How Commercial Pet Foods Can Go Wrong

Although the pet-food recall of 2007 will go down in history as one of the largest recalls so far, and potentially as one of the most deadly, there have been many pet-food recalls. In 2005 one manufacturer recalled its foods because aflatoxin (a toxin produced by a fungus) was found in its foods. In 2006 a rat poison was found in some pet foods. During the 2007 recalls, melamine (a chemical used in the making of plastic that is sometimes also used as a fertilizer) was found in many pet foods, and thousands of dogs and cats got sick and died.

What went wrong? Why did this happen? Unfortunately, those are hard questions to answer. Certainly one answer is that pet foods are now big business. Huge conglomerations now own pet-food companies that were once smaller, more intimate companies.

- Nestlé bought Purina and now controls all the Purina foods, including the Dog, Cat, Puppy, and Kitten Chows; Beneful; One; ProPlan; Fancy Feast; and more.
- MasterFoods owns Mars, Inc., which had previously bought Royal Canin, Pedigree, Waltham, Goodlife, Sensible Choice, and more.
- Plus, Del Monte bought Heinz, which produced Meow Mix, Gravy Train, 9 Lives, Nature's Recipe, Milk-Bone, and Pounce.

Whereas the small, individually owned pet-food companies were usually started by people who cared about pets and wanted the best for them, these huge businesses must answer to stock holders, who, of course, want to see those dividend checks.

Charlie Gillis and Anne Kingston, authors of "The Great Pet Food Scandal" (www.macleans.ca, April 30, 2007), say, "The story of how a tiny, shoestring operation in Toronto's western suburbs came to dominate its industry reflects the seismic shifts in the manufacturing food chain over the past three decades. Increasing power wielded by the margin-obsessed, cut-throat supermarket industry has forced manufacturers—such as Menu Foods—to source cheaper ingredients globally. Those forces have favored faceless giants—players capable of supplying myriad products demanded by retailers, retooling and remixing recipes as the orders came in. But as the Menu case demonstrates, the system also ensures a continent-wide catastrophe when something goes wrong. Marion Nestle, a professor in the department of nutrition, food studies, and public health at New York University, doesn't see the Menu tragedy as an aberration. Rather she calls it 'the tip of the iceberg.'"

Menu Foods imported ingredients, including wheat gluten, from China. Unfortunately, as we've seen, China's laws governing the growing and manufacturing of food are nothing like the laws of the United States. Hence, melamine and other things that have no business being in any food, for people or pets, have shown up with disastrous results. With inspection procedures being significantly less than perfect, these contaminated ingredients weren't caught until pets became sick and started dying.

But the U.S. food practices aren't ideal, either, by any means. For example, an animal that dies on the farm may not reach the slaughterhouse for days; although 4-D animals (diseased, dying, dead, or disabled) are not supposed to be used for human foods, they can be used in many pet-food formulations (as can roadkill and euthanized pets). Dead animals are contaminated with bacteria as well as with the normal process of decay. In addition, all the antibiotics and medications in that animal's system are still there too and certainly will affect the food quality.

Another risk of contamination in pet foods is the use of the remains of foods used in manufacturing foods for people. Catherine O'Driscoll said in her July 27, 2007, article, "Pet Food Unsafe Long Before Recall," "The United Kingdom's Pet Food Manufacturers Association, which includes many international conglomerates, states the following on its Web site in relation to pet foods, 'The industry's use of by-products from the human food and agricultural industries prevents the need for, and cost of, disposal.'" In other words, waste-removal costs are decreased because the wastes are being used in the making of pet foods.

In his article "Is Your Food Contaminated?" in the September 2007 issue of *Scientific American*, Mark Fischetti said, "Given the billions of food items that are packaged, purchased and consumed every day in the U.S., let alone the world, it is remarkable how few of them are contaminated." Preventing someone from contaminating a food product for people, livestock, or pets is a huge task and one that right now has barely been addressed. The food-supply chain is a huge one, and the number of steps the foods take varies, depending upon the item.

What Can Pet Owners Do about It?

Many pet owners who were worried about commercial pet-food practices have gone the natural route; they toss their dog a whole raw chicken or their cat an entire raw fish. Their thinking is that these foods are more natural and, as a result, healthier for their pets. We'll talk about raw foods in upcoming chapters, but just keep in mind that raw chicken is nothing like the clean, untainted birds wild canines caught thousands of years ago. Nor is the fish.

But, if you prefer to feed a commercial dog or cat food and yet wish your dog or cat to live a long, happy, healthy life, what can you do? There's a lot of bad news about commercial pet foods, but all pet foods are not bad. If you want to feed your pet a commercial pet food, the best thing you can is to become an educated consumer. Read as much as you can about dog and cat food from experts in the field, as you are doing here. Check out some of my resources listed in the appendix of this book.

In addition:

- Talk to your veterinarian. If your veterinarian has not studied nutrition, ask for a referral to someone local who has.
- If you do research on the Internet, before you take any information to heart, find out who the writer is and what his or her qualifications are. The Internet has produced millions of immediate experts and not all are as knowledgeable as we might think.
- If you are interested in a particular dog or cat food, call the manufacturer and ask questions. Do they know where their ingredients come from, or do they buy from a broker? If they know where the ingredients come from, they can maintain better quality control. Have they done any digestibility studies on the food? Ingredients can look great, but the dog or cat will suffer if he can't digest the food.

Commercial pet foods are readily available, and that is certainly in their favor. It's not hard to serve the foods, and most pets eat them quite readily. Although not always enforced as well as they could be, there are industry standards. And not all pet foods are horrible; there are some excellent quality pet foods available, and a few of them have been profiled in this book in the pet-food-comparison sidebars.

CHAPTER FOUR

The Old Is New Again

Home-Cooked Foods

Dog and cat owners have four choices as to how to feed their pets and all have their good and less-than-good points. Pet owners can feed their pet a commercial pet food and, in doing so, can choose from a wide variety of readily available foods. Pet owners can also offer their pet a commercial food, but they can add to its nutritional value by adding food supplements or a portion of a home-cooked food. In addition, many owners today are feeding a home-cooked-food or a raw-food diet.

We've already discussed the benefits and problems associated with commercial foods, and we'll discuss supplements in chapter 6, so let's take a look at home-cooked foods fed as a complete diet or as an addition to a commercial food, as there are certainly pros and cons to each of these as well. Raw-meat diets will be discussed in chapter 5.

Dog and cat owners investigate home-cooked diets for many reasons, such as illness or other health challenges. Other pet owners are worried about the quality of the commercial foods available. Many dog and cat owners are simply paying more attention to what they eat and want the same considerations for their pets. And then last, but certainly not least, many pet owners are rightfully concerned about what goes into commercial foods and have decided to trust only themselves to provide food for their pets.

The Pros and Cons of Home-Cooked Food

The primary benefit of a home-cooked dog or cat food is that you have complete and total control over the ingredients. You can choose what ingredients your dog or cat eats and the quality of those ingredients. If you want to avoid cereal grains, you can do that. If you want your dog to have more meat and your cat to have more fish, that's fine.

Unfortunately, this isn't always as easy as it sounds. Finding quality ingredients can be tough. You will also need to decide what kind of home-cooked diet you want to feed, plus you need to feel comfortable with the process of formulating your pet's diet.

Quality of Fruits and Vegetables

Determining the quality of the foods available to us today is hard. Those tomatoes at the grocery store look great, but where did they come from? Were they allowed to ripen on the vine or were they gassed to make them ripen after being picked? Oh, didn't you know tomatoes are gassed? Ripe tomatoes are soft and don't handle transportation from the fields to trucks to warehouses and then on to the stores. So they are picked green and then flooded with ethylene gas to make them ripen artificially. That's why those tomatoes you grow in the backyard taste so much better.

In addition, the vegetables and fruits may have been sprayed many times with pesticides and other chemicals during the growing process. The land, too, may be full of chemicals, pesticides, herbicides, and fertilizers, all of which can affect the growing crops.

Ideally, if you can find a local farmer's market where local produce is sold, you'll be more likely to find good-quality natural or organic fruits and vegetables. But even at a farmer's market, ask questions. Where was the produce grown? Has the produce been sprayed with pesticides, fertilizers, herbicides, or any other chemicals? And if it's important to you, ask if the produce was grown on an organic farm.

Although the terms *natural* and *organic* appear to have the same meanings for many people, in the food industry these are two different terms. *Natural* applies to foods that do not contain any artificial additives. That means no artificial or chemical preservatives, flavorings, or colorings.

There are very specific industry standards that must be met before the term *organic* can be used. Organic crops must be grown with no chemical pesticides or fertilizers. For organic meat, the animals cannot be genetically modified in any way, and no growth hormones can be used in the meat production.

Many grocery stores now have more organic produce. If the store where you normally shop doesn't have any, tell the produce manager or store manager that you are interested in this type of produce.

Plant Your Own Garden

If you can, plant your own garden. Or plant a community garden. Three friends and I get together and plant a garden every year. With four people (and a couple of some-times-unwilling teenagers) we can put in a good-sized garden and share the work. The food is for us and all our dogs, plus two of the people also have chickens and goats that can eat all of the spoiled produce. This year we put in zucchini, summer squash, crookneck squash, spaghetti squash, white corn, yellow sweet corn, several kinds of peppers, several kinds of tomatoes, artichokes, lots of pumpkins, watermelons, and cucumbers. We also put in some peppermint for our tea and catnip for the kitties. Because we did all the work, we could produce organic produce and not worry about any chemicals. We ate the produce fresh, and then canned and froze the rest for use during the winter.

Meat Quality

Dogs and cats must eat meat. Neither species is designed to be vegetarian, and although some dogs can eat other protein sources for a short period of time without detrimental effects, this should be done only under a veterinarian's supervision. Cats, however, are obligate carnivores; they must eat meat and will not thrive (or even survive) on a vegetarian diet.

Because meat is going to be the foundation of a home-cooked diet, the quality of meat that you feed your pets is important. If you can find a local butcher who gets his meat from local, known sources, that would be ideal. Many supermarkets today are bowing to pressures from consumers to offer better-quality meats. Consumers are more knowledgeable; we've read about antibiotics in livestock and growth hormones and filthy living conditions, and we want better-quality meats for ourselves and our pets.

Some pet owners have assured me that the meat they feed their dogs and cats is absolutely the best because they hunt on a regular basis and bring home wild game: deer, elk, rabbit, squirrel, and wild birds. Although it's true these animals will

Farm-Fresh Eggs

Eggs can be a valuable addition to a home-cooked diet for both dogs and cats because they offer complete proteins (with all the needed amino acids). Just as the quality of meat and produce can vary, depending upon the source, so can the quality of the eggs you buy.

Find a source of fresh eggs and buy those rather than the eggs that have been in the cooler at your grocery store for an unknown period of time. Not only do fresh eggs taste better, but if they are from free-range chickens, they will be cleaner. Commercially raised, caged chickens sit in cages piled one upon the other so that the urine and feces rain down on the birds below them.

Don't limit yourself to chicken eggs, either. Quail, duck, goose, and turkey eggs are also tasty and nutritious, and your pet will love them.

not contain growth hormones or antibiotics, it's not necessarily true that all of these animals are always healthier than those raised on a small family farm where people care about their animals' health. Wild animals are subjected to environmental toxins just as we are, plus some may be infested with parasites, both internal and external. In addition, the wild form of mad cow disease (bovine spongiform encephalopathy) has been spreading in herds of deer and elk in the United States. Animals with BSE should not be a part of the food chain.

Price

One of the common arguments against home-cooked pet-food diets is that it is expensive to cook for your pet at home. Fortunately, that's not necessarily true.

Keep in mind, the best commercial dog and cat foods are not cheap; the most inexpensive foods are the ones made with the most questionable ingredients. However, as we've seen in the past with various pet-food contaminations and recalls, sometimes not much separates the best from the worst, especially when both are produced at the same plant.

If you're cooking for your family and using good-quality ingredients, feeding your dog or cat those same foods will not affect your budget any more than it would to buy the better-quality dog or cat foods. In fact, you will probably save money.

Now, if your dog or cat has some food allergies and requires some different protein sources, like bison or duck, well, then the price tag could very well go up. However, talk to your local butcher. If you can guarantee him that you will buy so much bison or duck every week, he may just be able to get you a good deal. It never hurts to ask!

Food Preparation

If you fix your pet's meals while fixing your own, you'll only make one mess in the kitchen, and you can use many of the same ingredients. Home-cooked diets are definitely not as easy to fix and serve as most commercial foods are. You need to think ahead, plan, go shopping, and prepare the foods. However, many meals can be made ahead of time and refrigerated until it's time to serve the food. Often I will make a whole week's worth of meals ahead of time, especially if I know the coming week will be busy. Then I can freeze the meals and just pull them out the day before to thaw.

Travel

Many people today plan vacations and family reunions around places that allow pets; I know we do. If you travel with your pet, you need to be able to fix your pet's meals while traveling; commercial foods are much easier in that respect. But if you make several meals ahead of time and freeze them in airtight containers, you can then thaw and feed one meal at a time. Of course, if you're camping, you can cook your pet's food over the fire as you do your own!

Nutritional Content

Commercial foods have been tested as to their nutritional content, and vitamins and minerals are added to the formulas. Now granted, in many cases those vitamin and mineral additives are synthetic and not as easily metabolized as whole foods containing those vitamins and minerals. But the foods have been tested.

It is very difficult for a dog or cat owner to have a recipe tested as to its nutritional content. To prevent nutritional deficiencies, home-cooked diets should be varied from day to day, with different protein, fat, and carbohydrate sources. I'll guide you through the process, though, with time-tested recipes. In addition, the diets should be supplemented with whole foods containing vitamins and minerals, or a quality vitamin and mineral supplement; we'll discuss those and other important supplements in chapter 6.

Adding Home-Cooked Foods to Commercial Foods

If you want to improve your pet's nutrition, but aren't quite ready yet to take the leap to making all of your pet's food, you can continue to feed a commercial food and add some ingredients to it. By doing this, you can have the convenience and safety of a good commercial food, but yet feel as though you're adding to the food's nutritional value.

As we've discussed previously, the high temperatures required to process most commercial pet foods can potentially destroy many essential nutrients, including many vitamins, minerals, probiotics, and phytonutrients. You can put those nutrients back into the food by adding some home-cooked foods to the commercial food your pet eats. This must be done with care, however, as it is possible to upset the nutritional balance built in to the commercial food.

Start first of all with the best quality commercial dog or cat food you can find. Don't think that a dash of good homemade food will offset a cheap, poor-quality, commercial food—there's no way it can—because the commercial food will be the foundation you're building on.

The Honest Kitchen's "Preference"

Understanding that many people want to make their own dog food, The Honest Kitchen created a food that is designed to be used as a base for a home-cooked diet. Preference is made from alfalfa, sweet potatoes, cabbage, celery, apples, spinach, organic kelp, coconut, bananas, zucchini, and honey. At each meal, the dog owner can add meat, cooked or raw, to the formula and thus provide a well-balanced and nutritious meal. See www.thehonest kitchen.com.

Once you have a commercial food you trust, you need to start thinking about foods you can feed your dog or cat. Let's begin with leftovers; if you are eating healthy home-cooked meals yourself, there is absolutely no reason why you can't share some of those foods with your pet. If you have a roasted chicken or turkey, pull the last of the meat off the bird and use that meat for your pet's dinner and your lunch tomorrow. Are there some grated carrots left after fixing a dinner salad? Those are good food, too, for your pet. Is yogurt a part of your breakfast meal? That's just as good for your pet as it is for you.

Now, I understand we have been indoctrinated to think that leftovers are horrible foods for our pets. But who originated that line of thinking? The pet-food companies, of course, who told the veterinarians, who told pet owners! The major pet-food companies are very involved in promoting their foods to veterinarians and pet stores. They offer educational materials and even classes.

While foods that are healthy for us are generally healthy for our pets, there are some foods that should be avoided:

- chicken skin with fat
- the fat crust on a roast
- heavily spiced foods
- overly greasy foods
- chocolate
- cow's milk (yogurt and some cheeses are fine, and goat's milk and cheese are fine)
- refined white flours
- sugar (although some honey or molasses is okay)

Basically, if the food is good for us, it can also be good for our pets.

As you begin adding home-cooked foods to your pet's diet, you will gradually begin decreasing your pet's old food and adding some new foods.

- For the first two weeks, decrease the old food by 10 percent and add the same amount of new foods.
- If the dog or cat has tolerated the new foods well with no diarrhea, bloating, gas, or vomiting, then for weeks three and four, decrease the old foods by another 10 percent and increase the new foods by 10 percent.
- If the dog or cat is still doing well with no signs of gastrointestinal upset, then for weeks five and six, decrease the old foods by another 10 percent and increase the new foods by the same amount.

Continue until you are feeding 60 to 75 percent commercial food and 25 to 40 percent home-cooked foods.

Dairy Products in Your Pet's Diet

Many dogs and cats are lactose intolerant; they cannot digest cow's milk. Puppies and kitten have the enzyme lactase, which breaks down the sugar in milk called lactose. However, as a dog or a cat ages, it generally stops producing lactase. Then, when your dog or cat consumes cow's milk, the lactose is not digested and your pet may appear bloated, may have flatulence (gas), and may even have diarrhea.

However, even those pets who cannot drink cow's milk can often consume aged, fermented, or curdled products such as cheese, cottage cheese, and yogurt. Most animals that are lactose intolerant can easily tolerate goat's milk.

Since dairy products can be an excellent source of nutrition, you can see if your pet can tolerate some of these different foods by offering a half a teaspoon of them to a cat and a tablespoon for a fifty-pound dog. If your pet appears fine, offer a little more. However, if at any time your pet appears uncomfortable or has gas or diarrhea, cross that ingredient off your list of potential foods.

The ratio of the foods you add to your dog's or cat's commercial food can vary. However, if you're worried about disrupting the nutritional value of the food, here's a healthy guideline:

- animal protein (including meats, dairy, and eggs): roughly 75 percent for dogs and 80 percent for cats
- vegetables and fruits: no more than 15 percent for both dogs and cats
- grains and other foods: no more than 10 percent for dogs and 5 percent for cats

Good Foods

There are many foods you eat regularly that your dog and cat can eat.

- **Meats.** Beef, bison, venison, elk, rabbit, chicken, duck, turkey, and goose.
- **Fish.** Just about any deboned fish, including trout, bass, catfish, salmon, tuna, mackerel, or herring, as well as clams and oysters. Lobster if you want to share.
- **Dairy and eggs.** Goat's milk (no cow's milk), fresh goat cheeses, cottage cheese, yogurt, chicken eggs, duck eggs, quail eggs, and goose eggs.
- **Vegetables**. Carrots, spinach, broccoli, zucchini, squash of all kinds, pumpkin, green beans, kidney beans, sweet potatoes, yams, and potatoes.
- **Fruits.** Apple (no seeds), bananas, pears, and watermelon.
- **Cereal grains.** These are okay for specific needs or once in a while but should not be a large part of the diet: barley, oatmeal, wild or brown rice, and millet.
- **Other good foods.** Flaxseeds or flaxseed meal is very nutritious.

Use fish oils, safflower oil, sesame seed oil, or olive oil for some taste and fat content. Cats love salmon oil. Use tomatoes sparingly; they are nutritious, but the acid content can be tough on some digestive tracts.

You can add to this mixture any supplements that are needed or that you feel will benefit your pet's health. For more on supplements, see chapter 6.

This plan is very easy to implement; when you're cooking for the family, just make more than you're used to cooking. If I bake one chicken breast for my husband and one for me, I then add in one for each of the dogs. The same applies to the morning oatmeal or scrambled eggs, or the raw vegetables for a salad. An omelet with some chopped meat and lots of cheese is a canine and feline favorite at my house.

Sumptuous Sardines with Cat Food...............

This recipe is designed to be used as an add-on to a good-quality cat food; it should not be used alone.

> 1 six-ounce can of sardines in tomato sauce
> 1 egg, chicken, hard-boiled, crumbled, with shell
> 1/4 cup grated summer squash, steamed
> 1/4 cup yogurt, plain, regular

1. Put all of the ingredients in the blender or food processor and liquefy. Stop the machine and stir a couple of times to make sure all of the pieces (especially the eggshell) are finely ground.
2. Add one teaspoon to each meal to begin with; add slightly more later, as noted earlier.

Suggested daily supplements (see chapter 6) include the following:

- a good-quality natural vitamin and mineral supplement
- a 250 to 500 mg taurine supplement
- a fatty acid supplement, such as chicken fat, cod liver oil, salmon oil, fish oil, or safflower oil

- a bonemeal supplement: either natural bonemeal, finely ground eggshells, or a calcium lactate supplement
- a green-food supplement, such as blue-green algae, spirulina, or barley grass
- a health food blend, such as Tri-Natural Product's Missing Link for Cats

Supplements should be mixed in with all the foods as the food is served.

Variations (use the same amounts as for the ingredients being replaced):

- Use salmon in oil rather than sardines.
- Use a scrambled egg with a bit of cheese in it instead of a hard-boiled egg.
- Substitute goat's milk instead of yogurt. (Do not use cow's milk.)

This food will keep in the refrigerator for three to four days.

Chicken and Carrots with Dog Food . . . .

This nutritious recipe is designed to be used as an additive to a commercial dog food; it is not a complete diet.

....

^{1}/2 cup pasta
^{1}/4 cup carrots, raw, grated
^{1}/2 cup chicken hearts
^{1}/2 cup chicken, deboned
1 tablespoon molasses
^{1}/2 cup cottage cheese

....

1. Put the pasta in a saucepan, cover with water, and bring to a boil.
2. Cut the chicken hearts and chicken into bite-sized pieces and add to the water.
3. When the mixture has come to boil, turn the heat down, and add the grated carrots. Cook over a medium to low heat. If the water gets low, add just enough to cover the foods in the pan. Remove from stove when the meats are thoroughly cooked.
4. Add the molasses, mixing thoroughly but gently.
5. Divide the food (including the water it was cooked in) into as many meals as your dog is eating. Add a portion (a tablespoon for a fifty-pound dog) to his or her regular dog food to begin, along with a portion of the cottage cheese, and mix well.

Suggested supplements (see chapter 6) include the following:

- a good-quality natural vitamin and mineral supplement
- a fatty acid supplement, such as chicken fat, cod liver oil, salmon oil, fish oil, or safflower oil
- a bonemeal supplement: either natural bonemeal, finely ground eggshells, or a calcium lactate supplement
- a green-food supplement, such as blue-green algae, spirulina, or barley grass
- a health food blend, such as Springtime, Inc.'s Longevity or Tri-Natural Product's Missing Link

Add and mix in the supplements when the food is served. Refrigerate the remaining food.

Variations (use the same amounts as for the ingredients being replaced):

- Use beef instead of the chicken and chicken hearts.
- Use beef heart instead of the chicken and chicken heart.
- Use oatmeal instead of the pasta.
- Use yogurt instead of the cottage cheese.

Making a Home-Cooked Diet

Taking the leap to let commercial dog and cat foods go and to formulate a feeding plan for your pets is a huge responsibility. You, and you alone, will bear the weight of making sure your pet eats a healthful, balanced diet. His or her life and longevity depend on you. That said, you can do it, just as many other pet owners have. However, you cannot be cavalier about it; this does require some discipline and a plan to do it correctly.

- **Supplements.** You will need to add a couple of supplements to the home-cooked diet, including bonemeal for both dogs and cats, and taurine for cats. We'll discuss which ones are important in more detail in chapter 6. The supplements will both add to the pet's diet and help prevent any nutritional deficiencies.
- **Vary the proteins.** It's important to vary the proteins used in your pet's diet. By changing these, you can add different tastes to your pet's food, but more importantly, you add extra nutrition to the diet. Different proteins offer a variety of amino acids, enzymes, vitamins, and minerals.
- **Steam the veggies.** Vegetables and other plant products (excluding fruits) should be lightly steamed or cooked with the recipe. Overcooking can decrease the nutrition

of the food, however, so steaming the vegetables for just a few seconds will make nutrients more digestible to your carnivore without overcooking.

- **Cook the cereal grains.** Although cereal grains are not natural foods to dogs or cats, some (not all) can provide some nutrition if fed wisely and in very limited amounts. Cereal grains should always be cooked, however, to make them more digestible.
- **Quality.** Find the best quality ingredients you can, meat, eggs, and produce.
- **Calorie requirements.** Just as individual people have very specific calorie needs, so do our pets. However, to find a starting point, most fifty-pound adult dogs who are pets (going for a walk every day and playing ball in the afternoon) need about 1,200 to 1,400 calories per day. Most adult, indoor cats who weigh between nine and ten pounds will need 350 to 375 calories per day. If your pet gains or loses weight, you can make changes to the recipes to increase or decrease the calorie count.

This book contains a wide variety of recipes with many different ingredients. Some of the recipes are for specific life stages or health situations (nursing mothers or pets with heart disease, for example), but many of the others are for adult, healthy pets.

Choose a recipe (or two or three) that you can make on a regular basis. Each recipe offers two or three variations so that you can change certain ingredients but so the recipe will still work. By using two or three recipes plus their variations, you can feed your pet well and be assured your pet is getting the best nutrition possible. Although some pets may hesitate when initially offered a different ingredient, as they get used to eating these new foods that hesitation usually disappears.

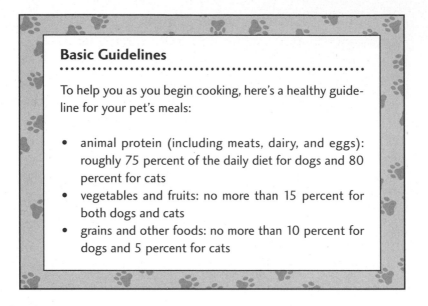

Basic Guidelines

To help you as you begin cooking, here's a healthy guide-line for your pet's meals:

- animal protein (including meats, dairy, and eggs): roughly 75 percent of the daily diet for dogs and 80 percent for cats
- vegetables and fruits: no more than 15 percent for both dogs and cats
- grains and other foods: no more than 10 percent for dogs and 5 percent for cats

Tips for Feeding a Home-Cooked Diet

Obviously you're creating a home-cooked diet for your dog or cat because you want the best for your pet. To help you keep him at his best, here are a few tips that sum up what we've been saying about these diets:

- **Cook the meats.** We'll discuss raw-food diets in chapter 5, and they have their own protocols for safety that must be followed. So unless you specifically want a raw-food diet, cook your pet's meats.
- **Vegetables should be steamed.** Most vegetables and plant products (except fruits) should be at least steamed. Steaming for a minute or two will not destroy all the phytonutrients but will help break cellulose walls so that they are more digestible. If the vegetables are served raw, they should be chopped or grated into very small pieces.

- **Grains should be cooked.** Cereal grains should be thoroughly cooked so that the animal can digest them.
- **Add supplements wisely.** Adding supplements to your pet's food will fill in the nutritional gaps that might occur once in a while. Supplements can also add beneficial nutrients to the individual recipes that you're using. Chapter 6 discusses supplements; add them to your home-cooked diet.

Foods to Avoid

Some foods should be avoided, as they can either be toxic to our pets, are not readily digested, or may simply cause some gastrointestinal upsets.

- **Avocado.** Thousands of dogs in California eat avocados every day, usually by picking up the fruit that has fallen from the tree. These dogs rarely have a problem (other than from the high fat content), but some reactions have been seen. If you would like to add avocado to your dog's or cat's diet, talk to your veterinarian first.
- **Chocolate.** Although cats are not attracted to chocolate, dogs often are and will readily eat it. Unfortunately, it can be toxic to dogs and cats. No chocolate.
- **Citrus.** Most dogs and cats are not attracted to citrus fruits and can't digest them well, even if they wanted to eat them. You can share a section of orange once in a while but otherwise, go easy on the citrus.
- **Grapes and raisins.** Dogs enjoy the sweet taste of grapes (cats do not have taste receptors for sweets), but don't offer either grapes or raisins to dogs or cats; they will make your pet sick.

continues

continued

- **Grease.** Pull the thick fat off your meats and toss it. Your dog or cat might like to eat some or all of it, but that much will give them diarrhea. Dogs and cats need some fat in the diet, but very few need that much fat. No bacon grease or hamburger grease, except what little remains in the meat after you drain the meat well.
- **Seasoned meats.** Avoid any meats that are chemically preserved, salted, smoked, or sugared. Avoid highly spiced meats, too.
- **Spices.** Very few dogs or cats are attracted to heavily spiced foods, and if they were to eat these foods, a bellyache might be the result later. It's best to keep spicy foods away from your pet.
- **Sugar.** Cats are not attracted to sugar or sweet foods, but many dogs are. Honey can be used in some recipes for both species for a touch of sweet, as can molasses. Plus both of these are a good source of minerals. However, refined white sugar should be avoided.
- **Wheat.** Most dogs and cats do not digest wheat well at all, in any of its forms. In addition, it causes a lot of allergy problems. Avoid wheat, wheat flour, middlings, germ, or bran.

If your pet has eaten something he or she shouldn't have (the box of chocolate candy is empty, and no one else was around), call your veterinarian right away. Some symptoms of gastrointestinal upset include a bloated appearance, flatulence (gas), vomiting, or diarrhea. However, if any of these foods were available to your pet (even if he sneaked them on his own) and his behavior has changed in any way (lethargic, restless, or uneasy), call your veterinarian.

Recipes for Cats

Chicken and Tuna Delight . . . .

Although most people wouldn't think of combining two such different meats as chicken and tuna for one of their own meals, cats love this combination.

This recipe makes one day's food supply (about 450 calories) for an average, indoor, ten- to twelve-pound cat.

²/₃ cup chicken, raw, deboned, cut into strips
1 three-ounce can of tuna in oil
1 chicken egg, small, hard-boiled, shell removed
2 tablespoons oatmeal, cooked (left over from
    breakfast is fine)
2 tablespoons wheatgrass

1. Steam or bake the chicken until done yet still tender. Cut or shred the meat into very small, bite-sized pieces for your cat.
2. While the chicken is cooking, break up the hard-boiled egg into a small bowl. Crumble it well.
3. Cut the wheatgrass into small pieces and place on a paper plate or microwave-safe plate. Cover with a damp paper towel and microwave for ten seconds. (If you don't have a microwave, dip the wheatgrass into boiling water for about five seconds, then remove.)
4. Combine cooked chicken, tuna, oatmeal, and grass in the bowl with the crumbled egg. Mix well.

5. Divide into two, three, four, or five meals (depending upon how many your cat is used to eating each day) and refrigerate the meals not being served immediately.

Suggested daily supplements (see chapter 6) include the following:

- a good-quality natural vitamin and mineral supplement
- a 250 to 500 mg taurine supplement
- a bonemeal supplement: either natural bonemeal, finely ground eggshells, or a calcium lactate supplement
- a green-food supplement, such as blue-green algae, spirulina, or barley grass
- a health food blend, such as Tri-Natural Product's Missing Link for Cats

Supplements should be added as the food is served.

Variations (unless otherwise noted, use the same amounts as for the ingredients being replaced):

- If you have access to quail eggs, add two to three hard-boiled quail eggs (no shells) instead of one chicken egg. Or hard-boil a duck, goose, or turkey egg, remove the shell, and just use half of the egg in each day's recipe.
- Instead of wheatgrass, you can use any grass grown indoors for your cat, including oat grass, millet, or bluegrass. Do *not* use sorghum or sudangrass, as both are poisonous to cats.
- Substitute turkey for chicken.
- Substitute salmon for tuna.

This food will remain good in the refrigerator for two to three days.

Seafood Special . . . .

This tasty, appealing recipe has 350 calories and is a good recipe for a ten-pound, indoor adult cat.

1 cup oysters, fresh or canned, drained
1 three-ounce can of tuna in water, drained
  (but save water in case it's needed)
1 egg, chicken, large, hard-boiled and crumbled
2 tablespoons carrot, grated, steamed

1. Put all the ingredients in a food processor and liquefy until a thick paste. Add a tiny bit of the oyster or tuna water if needed for processing.
2. Put mixture in an airtight bowl and store in the refrigerator.
3. Divide into as many meals as your cat is used to eating.

Suggested daily supplements include the following:

- a good-quality natural vitamin and mineral supplement
- a taurine supplement
- a fatty acid supplement, such as chicken fat, cod liver oil, salmon oil, fish oil, or safflower oil
- a bonemeal supplement: either natural bonemeal, finely ground eggshells, or a calcium lactate supplement
- a green-food supplement, such as blue-green algae, spirulina, or barley grass
- a health food blend, such as Tri-Natural Product's Missing Link for Cats

Supplements should be added as the food is served.

Recipes for Dogs

Chicken Stew. . . . .

This recipe is wonderful for the slow cooker; put the recipe in the crock pot before you leave for work and it's ready when you come home. It supplies a full day's worth of meals for a fifty-pound dog.

3 cups chicken, raw, diced into small pieces
$1/2$ cup potato, diced into small pieces
$1/4$ cup celery
$1/4$ cup parsley
$1/4$ cup carrots, grated
$1/4$ cup broccoli florets, diced
1 tablespoon flaxseeds

1. Brown the chicken, and when the meat is browned, transfer it to a slow cooker.
2. Add the remaining ingredients and add enough water to just cover them.
3. Put your slow cooker on low and let it cook all day.
4. When serving, include the cooking water, as it is rich in nutrients. Divide into two meals and store in the refrigerator.

Suggested supplements include the following:

- a good-quality natural vitamin and mineral supplement
- a fatty acid supplement, such as chicken fat, cod liver oil, salmon oil, fish oil, or safflower oil

- a bonemeal supplement: either natural bonemeal, finely ground eggshells, or a calcium lactate supplement
- a green-food supplement, such as blue-green algae, spirulina, or barley grass
- a health food blend, such as Springtime, Inc.'s Longevity or Tri-Natural Product's Missing Link

Supplements should be added as the food is served.

Gina's Beef and Cheese . . . .

Gina, a petite, feminine rottweiler, is picky about her food, so when we find, during our taste tests, a recipe Gina likes, well, then it's all hers!

This nutritious recipe supplies about 1,200 calories and is good for most forty- to fifty-pound active adult house dogs who go for a walk every day, play ball, and do some obedience training but are otherwise relatively calm.

> 2 cups beef, ground, cooked
> 2 eggs, chicken
> 1/2 cup squash, butternut, precooked
> 1/2 cup potato, russet or red, precooked, with skin
> 1/4 cup cheese, cheddar, grated
> 1 tablespoon sesame oil

1. Preheat oven to 350 degrees.
2. Place the cooked ground beef in a bowl and break up any chunks.
3. Cut the precooked squash and potato into small pieces (smaller than bite-sized for your dog is best). Add to the ground beef.

4. Add the eggs, cheese, and oil, and then mix well.
5. Divide the mixture in half and shape each half into a small meatloaf. Put into a mini meatloaf pan (5½ inches by 3¼ by 1⅞ is a common size).
6. Bake for about thirty minutes or until a meat thermometer shows the meat is done inside (at least 160 degrees).
7. Remove pans from oven, let cool, and store in the refrigerator. Each pan is one meal for a dog who is fed twice a day.

Suggested supplements (see chapter 6) include the following:

- a good-quality natural vitamin and mineral supplement
- a bonemeal supplement: either natural bonemeal, finely ground eggshells, or a calcium lactate supplement
- a green-food supplement, such as blue-green algae, spirulina, or barley grass
- a health food blend, such as Springtime, Inc.'s Longevity or Tri-Natural Product's Missing Link

Supplements should be added as the food is served.

Food should remain good in the refrigerator for three to four days.

Variations (using the same quantities as for the original ingredients):

- Substitute bison for the beef.
- Substitute venison or elk for the beef.
- Use duck, goose, or turkey eggs instead of chicken eggs.
- Use sweet potatoes or yams instead of russet potatoes.
- Use grated zucchini instead of butternut squash.
- Use mozzarella cheese instead of cheddar.

Bison and Millet . . . .

This recipe is made with two rather unusual ingredients—bison and millet—and is very good for dogs showing signs of food allergies. However, this tasty and easy recipe is not limited just to allergic dogs; it's nutritious and about 1,400 calories, which is good for an active, fifty-pound adult dog.

> 2 cups raw bison
> 1 cup millet, pearled
> 1 cup green beans, fresh, chopped
> 1 tablespoon sesame oil or olive oil

1. Put the millet on to cook according to package directions and cook until well done. Drain off the excess water and set the cooked grains aside.
2. Cut the meat into bite-sized pieces. Brown until done but still tender.
3. With the heat on low under the meat, add the cooked millet and fresh green beans. Stir well and cook until the green beans are tender.
4. Turn off the heat and add the oil, stirring until well mixed.
5. Divide the mixture into two serving portions and store in airtight containers. Refrigerate until time to serve.

Suggested supplements (see chapter 6) include the following:

- a good-quality natural vitamin and mineral supplement
- a bonemeal supplement: either natural bonemeal, finely ground eggshells, or a calcium lactate supplement
- a green-food supplement, such as blue-green algae, spirulina, or barley grass

A health food blend, such as Springtime, Inc.'s Longevity or Tri-Natural Product's Missing Link

Supplements should be added as the food is served.

Variations (using the same quantities as for the original ingredients):

- Use venison or elk instead of bison.
- Use salmon, mackerel, or cod instead of bison.
- Use duck or goose instead of bison.
- Use oatmeal, amaranth, or barley instead of millet.
- Use red kidney beans instead of green beans.
- Use broccoli florets instead of green beans.

Beef and Cheddar . . . .

This nutritious recipe supplies about 1,200 calories and is good for most forty- to fifty-pound adult house dogs.

> 2 cups beef, ground, cooked
> 2 eggs, chicken
> 1/2 cup zucchini, grated
> 1/2 cup potato, russet or red
> 1/2 cup cheese, cheddar, grated
> 1 tablespoon safflower oil

1. Preheat oven to 350 degrees.
2. Place the cooked ground beef in a bowl and break up any chunks.
3. Cut the potato into small pieces (smaller than bite-sized for your dog is best). Add the potato and the grated zucchini to the ground beef.
4. Add the eggs, cheese, and oil, and then mix well.

5. Divide the mixture in half and shape each half into a small meatloaf. Put into a mini meatloaf pan (5½ inches by 3¼ by 1⅞ is a common size).

6. Bake for about thirty minutes or until a meat thermometer shows the meat is done inside (at least 160 degrees).

7. Remove pans from oven, let cool, and store in the refrigerator. Each pan is one meal for a dog who is fed twice a day.

Suggested daily supplements include the following:

- a good-quality natural vitamin and mineral supplement
- a bonemeal supplement; either natural bonemeal, finely ground eggshells, or a calcium lactate supplement
- a green-food supplement, such as blue-green algae, spirulina, or barley grass
- a health food blend, such as Springtime, Inc.'s Longevity or Tri-Natural Product's Missing Link

Supplements should be added as the food is served.

Food should remain good in the refrigerator for three to four days. If you double or triple the recipe, freeze any food that won't be fed within four days.

Turkey, Egg, and Sweet Potato . . . .

This recipe makes one day's worth of meals, about 1,200 calories, for a forty- to fifty-pound house dog who goes for walks and plays ball, but is otherwise relatively calm.

. . . .

2½ cups turkey, ground or shredded
    muscle meat
1 egg, chicken, hard-boiled, shelled

1 cup sweet potato, finely chopped
1/4 cup broccoli florets, finely chopped
1/4 cup spinach, fresh, finely chopped
2 teaspoons safflower oil
1/4 cup yogurt, plain, regular

....

1. If you're using leftover turkey, shred the meat into small pieces. If you're using fresh ground turkey, brown the meat.
2. Put the sweet potato, spinach, and broccoli on a microwave-safe plate or a paper plate and cover with a wet paper towel. Steam until the potato is tender.
3. Combine all the ingredients except the yogurt, making sure all of the ingredients are well mixed.
4. Divide into meals and store in the refrigerator in an airtight container.
5. When serving, add a portion of the yogurt to each meal.

Suggested daily supplements include the following:

- a good-quality natural vitamin and mineral supplement
- a bonemeal supplement: either natural bonemeal, finely ground egg shells, or a calcium lactate supplement
- a green-food supplement, such as blue-green algae, spirulina, or barley grass
- a health food blend, such as Springtime, Inc.'s Longevity or Tri-Natural Product's Missing Link

Supplements should be added as the food is served.

This food will be good in the refrigerator for two to three days.

Variations (using the same quantities as for the original ingredients):

- Use chicken instead of turkey.
- Use cottage cheese instead of yogurt.
- Use romaine, bok choy, Swiss chard, collard greens, or other dark green vegetables instead of spinach and broccoli.

CHAPTER FIVE

All about Raw-Food Diets

Raw-food diets have gained in popularity over the past decade, and more and more people are exploring this feeding option for their pets. One of the more popular raw food regimes is BARF (Bones and Raw Foods), which was begun by an Australian veterinarian, Dr. Ian Billinghurst. Although Dr. Billinghurst's program is one of the best known, there are many different raw-food diets (also called biologically appropriate raw foods).

Most of the pet owners who begin feeding their pets a raw-food diet do it because they have been disappointed by a commercial pet-food product. Perhaps their dog or cat developed some health problems related to the food, or their pet failed to thrive. Some have found themselves discouraged by several commercial dog or cat foods. Perhaps the pet became sick due to a contaminated food, or perhaps the owner has simply done some research on the commercial pet-food industry and is disillusioned.

The artificial additives present in commercial pet foods concern dog and cat owners, too, including the synthetic vitamins and minerals, the artificial flavors, colors, and, of course, the preservatives. This, too, should be a cause for concern. Many of the additives, especially preservatives such as BHA, BHT, and ethoxyquin, have been linked to health problems, including kidney and liver disease.

The theory behind feeding raw foods to dogs and cats is that these foods are more natural than the commercial pet foods are. That is certainly true with many of the commercial foods, especially those full of cereal grains; a bobcat will never harvest rice to add to his rabbit dinner, and a wolf isn't going to pick some barley to mix with his caribou. But as with all methods of feeding our pets, there are pros and cons to feeding a raw-food diet. A raw-food diet can be wonderful for your pet, nutritious and healthful, or it can make you and your pet deathly ill.

Some Serious
Concerns about Raw-Food Diets

Raw foods are definitely more natural, both for our pets and for ourselves. Thousands of years ago, raw foods were what we all ate. However, just because it's natural, does that make it better for us and for our pets? This is a highly debated topic; below you'll find some of the benefits and drawbacks of feeding raw foods to your pets.

Wild Canines and Felines Eat Raw Foods

Proponents of the raw-food diets, such as Dr. Billinghurst and Tom Lonsdale, Australian veterinarian and author of

Work Wonders (Rivetco P/L, 2005), state that a diet such as this contains all of the nutrients a carnivore requires for good health, including vitamins, minerals, probiotics, and phytonutrients.

Many of the proponents of raw-food diets, including the Drs. Billinghurst and Lonsdale, like to compare our domesticated dogs and cats to wild predators. They say that these animals hunted for themselves and obviously thrived on raw foods. Granted, many of the behaviors our dogs and cats have are similar to their wild cousins, but our pets have been domesticated for thousands of years. That's like comparing ourselves, today, to Neanderthals.

Today's dogs and cats are descended from their wild cousins and still bear a resemblance to those wild predators, but they are also far different. John Burns, BVMS MRCVS, said, "Dogs were domesticated about 15,000 years ago (and cats about 6,000 years ago). For dogs, that's about 3,000 to 7,500 generations." He added, "Man has had fire for hundreds of thousands of years and has been cooking for much of that time. It is very likely that the first domesticated dogs were introduced to cooked foods very early in the relationship." Dr. Burns also said that those early people selected and bred dogs who best suited their purposes—guarding, herding, hunting—as well as the dogs who thrived on the foods the people ate.

Since that time we have also bred for extremes: giant size, minuscule size, short coats, long coats, big eyes, short muzzles, long legs, short legs, and no tails. Other things have tagged along with those changes, including a lack of hunting ability, a lessened prey drive, an infantile dependence on people, and much more. Our dogs and cats may be relatives of those wild predators, but they are also vastly different.

Is Raw Meat Safe?

Proponents of raw-food diets state that our dogs and cats are biologically able to eat raw meats and handle the possible contamination of the meats because their ancestors were able to. Granted, dogs and cats are carnivores and need to eat a diet comprised primarily of meat (and cats must eat meat). Their bodies digest meats more readily than most plant products. That's true, but as noted earlier, today's meat hasn't been raised in the wild and mostly comes from feedlots.

In addition, we have no idea if wild predators ever suffer from a stomachache or are poisoned by eating spoiled meat. As Shawn Messonnier, DVM, said, "To say that wild animals suffer no ill effects from eating raw meat is ignorant and presupposes we know everything that happens to every wild animal."

Both wild and domestic meat animals can carry diseases and parasites, some of which can be transmitted to the animal that comes into contact with it, both through hunting and touching the animal or consuming the animal's flesh. Domestic animals crowded into feedlots or cages can be sickly, malnourished, diseased, and parasitic. In addition, animals raised on factory farms will be full of growth hormones and antibiotics. The meat from diseased animals should never be fed to our pets as raw meat; it is far too dangerous.

The meat that you feed your pet, especially raw meats, must be from healthy animals and known sources where it has been handled correctly. We'll discuss this in more depth as we go along.

Your Pet's Immune System Can't Handle Everything

Feeding your pet raw meats means you have to find, purchase, and handle raw meats. You need to be able to prepare the meats and feed them to your pet while maintaining the levels of cleanliness so that you, your family, and your pets remain healthy.

Proponents argue that the digestive tracts of carnivores fed a natural raw-food diet can eliminate any bacteria found in the meat, and for the most part that's true. Healthy dogs and cats are less likely to become sick because their immune systems are strong. However, variables exist, and if the chicken is infected with salmonella or the beef is infected with E. coli, then the dog or cat who eats it could potentially become very ill, no matter how strong the immune system.

Bacterial contamination occurs all the time in meat-processing plants, otherwise known as slaughterhouses. The animals are producing urine and feces, which can contaminate the meat. The dirty conditions of the slaughterhouse can also create contamination problems. Ordinarily, the temperatures that meats are cooked at will destroy most of the bacteria, but if you're feeding raw meats to your pet and are handling that meat, the contamination risk is huge.

Salmonella bacteria usually infect meats during the slaughtering process when animal feces come into contact with the meat. When contaminated meat is eaten either raw or undercooked, the person or animal eating the meat will develop diarrhea and stomach cramps and become very sick. Intravenous fluids are needed to prevent dehydration; antibiotic therapy is necessary to reduce the bacterial levels; and supportive care is necessary to assist the person, dog, or cat as he or she recovers. If the salmonella bacteria move through the bloodstream to other organs, the infection may be fatal.

Escherichia coli, or E. coli, is one of the bacteria that normally lives in the large intestines of mammals. When working as it should, E. coli assists in the production of vitamin K and helps with food absorption and in waste production. However, when

Raw-Meat-Handling Tips

To keep your family and your pets safe, you must first of all find a good source of raw meats and we'll discuss that a little bit later in this chapter. Here are some meat-handling tips:

- When shopping, pick up meats last, check out, and then go straight home.
- If you can't go straight home or have a drive of ten to fifteen minutes or more, carry the meat home in an ice chest filled with ice.
- Store meats in the refrigerator set at forty degrees Fahrenheit or colder.
- Meats will generally remain good for three days in the refrigerator.
- Meats can be frozen (with the freezer set at 0 degrees or colder) for three to four months.
- Defrost meats in the refrigerator, never at room temperature.
- Don't let raw meat touch other foods that will not be cooked.
- Dip the meat in a mild 2 percent bleach and water solution to kill any bacteria, or in a grapefruit-seed extract and water solution. (This can be found at health food stores.)
- Wash your hands with soap and hot water before and after touching raw meats.
- Wash counters, cutting boards, knives, utensils, and other surfaces that have been touched by raw meat with bleach and water.

animals are slaughtered, their meat can become contaminated with E. coli when feces or the contents of the large intestine come into contact with the meat. If the meat is stored incorrectly or is served raw or undercooked, then an overgrowth of E. coli can result. The dog or cat will show gastrointestinal upset, including diarrhea, vomiting, restlessness, or lethargy, and will run a fever. Antibiotic therapy is essential to treat E. coli. Unfortunately, excessive use of antibiotics as a food additive in livestock has created growing strains of antibiotic-resistant E. coli.

Are Raw Bones Safe?

The majority of the raw-food diets encourage the feeding of raw bones to both dogs and cats. Proponents, including Dr. Tom Lonsdale, say that these raw bones add nutrients to the pet's food and help clean the teeth as the pet chews on them. Anyone who has watched a dog chew on a big beef knucklebone or a cat gnawing on a chicken neck has to admit that our pets enjoy those bones. In addition, the bones can be a vital part of the pet's balanced nutrition, as meat contains lots of phosphorus and no calcium; the bones contain calcium but no phosphorus. Your pet needs a balance of these two minerals.

Unfortunately, these bones can hurt our pets. Dogs and cats can break their teeth on bones. My now eight-year-old dog, Riker, only weighs fifty pounds but is a power chewer and has broken two of his molars chewing on raw beef knucklebones. Both teeth had to be pulled.

Bones can cause other problems too. Robert S. Goldstein, VMD, a practicing holistic veterinarian for more than thirty years, and Susan J. Goldstein, also an expert on the holistic needs of dogs and cats, wrote in their book, *The Goldsteins'*

Wellness & Longevity Program (TFH, 2005), "While many holistic veterinarians say that in most instances there are no problems feeding raw bones, there are many reports of impactions of bones in the mouth, throat, and in the large bowel, as well as perforations of the intestines."

However, if you do want to feed bones, give raw, not cooked bones. Feeding your pet raw bones is one way to reduce the dangers of bones, as the raw bones are less apt to splinter than cooked bones. You can also offer your pet smaller, softer bones, such as those in chicken or turkey necks—just give your pet the entire neck. If you want to give your dog larger bones, supervise carefully, and take the bone away if he or she is breaking it into large slivers that could be swallowed.

Another way to add the nutritional benefit of the bones to the diet is to grind the bones into a powder using either a powerful food processor, a meat grinder, or asking your butcher to do this for you. This eliminates the dangers of impaction and perforation.

Just Be Careful

I have met some absolutely gorgeous, healthy, vital dogs and cats who eat only raw-food diets. These foods can be wonderful for our pets, but, just like commercial foods and home-cooked diets, they must be fed to our pets with knowledge and care. So think about this carefully before you do anything, and don't hesitate to talk to a holistic veterinarian, too, and ask for his or her thoughts.

If at any time while feeding raw foods you believe your dog or cat might have a problem, talk to your veterinarian. Dr. Messonnier said, "Any signs of illness as a result of feeding raw meat diets should be evaluated by a veterinarian at once."

Some signs of a potential problem might include:

- Any significant, sudden weight loss can be a sign of a bacterial infection, not enough food, malnutrition, or a problem digesting the food.
- Restlessness, anxiety, or biting at the abdomen can be a sign of an intestinal blockage, an impacted bone, extreme gas, or another gastrointestinal problem.
- Diarrhea and vomiting can be symptoms of many problems. Call you vet if either is extreme or lasts for more than twelve hours.
- Blood in the feces, vomit, or urine can be signs of several serious problems; call your vet right away.

Many dogs and cats will do very well when changed from a commercial dry food to a raw-food diet. The coat will shine, they will be bright eyed and happy and will eat with gusto. However, because there can be potential problems with this feeding regime, keep an eye on your pet and watch for any changes that could signal a health crisis.

It's All about Quality

The quality of a raw-food diet is based on the quality of the meats, eggs, and cheeses, and produce. If these are not fresh, clean, uncontaminated with bacteria, and grown with care, then the whole diet will fail and your pets will suffer because of it.

Free-Range Meats

Unfortunately, today, far too many livestock animals spend their lives in horrible conditions, packed into crowded cages or pens. Urine and feces pile up, and the animals cannot remain clean. Believe it or not, no animal wants to stand in his own urine and feces; when given a choice they will move away from a favorite resting spot to relieve themselves. In feedlots and cages, even the animals' food sources are polluted with urine and feces. Obviously the meat from these animals should be cooked.

Luckily, though, not all livestock raisers believe that this is fair to the animals or the consumers, and many are raising free-range livestock. These animals—chickens, ducks, geese, turkeys, goats, sheep, cattle, and bison—are allowed room to roam. They are clean and can move away from urine and feces. In addition, these animals are also allowed to eat more naturally; the chickens scratch for bugs, and the sheep and cattle graze.

Finding these sources of quality meats doesn't have to be difficult. I suggest you talk to a local butcher and find out if he knows any suppliers. The meat may initially be more expensive, but if you can assure him that you will buy so much per week, he may be willing to make you a deal. You can also go to Local Harvest online, at www.localharvest.org, and search for local markets, farmers, and farmer's markets by zip code. Since more people are concerned about quality foods, it's getting easier to find these foods.

Fresh Eggs

Fresh eggs from chickens who are allowed to forage daily and who are fed good-quality foods are superior to grocery-store eggs both in taste and nutrition.

Think about other types of eggs, too. We have a half a dozen geese, and each spring we have two or three geese eggs each

Meat and Egg Safety

If you have any doubts at all about the safety of the meat you buy, do something about it before feeding it to your dog or cat. The Goldsteins say, "You may want to lightly steam the meat, thereby reducing the potential for surface contamination." Dr. Shawn Messonnier recommends, "Thoroughly wash the meat at home."

If you are uncertain about the quality of the eggs you have bought, cook them before feeding them to your pet. Eggs, too, can harbor bacteria, and in any case, hard-boiled eggs are still very good nutrition.

day. These are wonderful for baking, for omelets, and our dogs and cats enjoy the variety too. You may be able to find duck, geese, turkey, and quail eggs that are raised locally.

If you don't know anyone with fresh eggs, see if there is a local farmer's market in your area. Many times you can find fresh eggs there.

Fresh Produce

Vegetables and fruits are a part of the raw-food diet, just as they are a home-cooked diet. Ideally, these should be grown without pesticides, insecticides, herbicides, and other dangerous chemicals. If you can't grow your own, buy from a local organic or natural farmer.

Getting Started

If you have decided that you would like to try and switch your pets over to a raw-food diet, do so gradually. If you simply toss out that commercial dog or cat food and hand your pet a chunk of meat, your dog or cat may end up in gastrointestinal distress. Oh, he'll probably eat the meat; most do. But your dog may try and gulp the chunk of meat, perhaps afraid that you'll change your mind and take it back, and could potentially choke himself. Or his intestinal tract may rebel against the unknown food.

So begin this slowly. Listed at the end of this chapter are a couple of easy recipes labeled transitional recipes—one for dogs and one for cats—and just add a spoonful a day (a teaspoon for cats and a tablespoon for a fifty-pound dog) to your pet's regular food. If your pet's feces are fine, and there's no diarrhea or other sign of gastrointestinal upset, then gradually, over a few weeks, decrease the commercial food and add more raw foods. You can continue until your pet is eating a complete raw-food diet.

The ratio of the ingredients in a raw-food recipe can vary, and there's no problem if they vary from day to day. However, overall, here's a healthy guideline:

- animal protein (including meats, dairy, and eggs): roughly 75 percent for dogs and 80 percent for cats
- vegetables and fruits: no more than 15 percent for both dogs and cats
- grains and other foods: no more than 10 percent for dogs and 5 percent for cats

You can add to this mixture any supplements that are needed or that you feel will benefit your pet's health, and we'll talk about those more in chapter 6.

A More Gradual Transition

Some pets have a hard time switching to a raw-food diet. Older pets, dogs and cats with illnesses or gastrointestinal disease, or those with immune system problems may need a more gradual introduction to a raw-food diet than the recipes listed later in this chapter can give them.

Signs that the dog or cat is not tolerating the changes well may include the following:

- flatulence (gas)
- diarrhea
- vomiting
- decrease in appetite (even for the new foods)
- scratching, itching, biting, or licking at the paws or base of the tail
- increase in symptoms of the pet's original health problem or disease

For these pets, introduce first a homemade diet that is cooked, such as the ones listed in the last chapter or those listed in chapter 10, for pets with special needs.

Change gradually, over three to four weeks, from the food the pet is used to eating to the home-cooked diet. Then, after transitioning to a home-cooked diet, let the pet get used to eating these new foods, even for three to four months, and then begin making some minor changes toward a raw-food diet.

- Feed the home-cooked meal, but as a treat during the day, offer a raw chicken neck for the dog to chew on and devour. Offer a cat a quarter of a chicken neck.

- Give the cat a small piece of raw fish as a treat.
- Add a raw beef knucklebone to the dog's diet three to four times per week as an after-meal snack.
- For cats and dogs, cook the meat in the recipe less, so that it's cooked on the outside but red in the middle.

When the pet can tolerate these changes with no gastro-intestinal upset, gradually begin changing to a raw-food diet by cooking the ingredients less and including more raw foods. It is also very important to work with your veterinarian during this changeover period, especially if your dog or cat is suffering from an illness.

Feeding Whole Carcasses

Tom Lonsdale, a proponent of feeding dogs raw foods, and several other raw-food enthusiasts also encourage feeding the dog the entire carcass of animals including squirrels, rabbits, chickens, and rats. During deer-hunting season, he suggests collecting and then freezing the leftovers (such as head and offal) from hunters who have shot and butchered their deer. He says the entire body has value to the dog, including the meat, bones, cartilage, and hair or feathers.

This type of feeding is usually not applicable to cats. Although many cats can learn to eat raw meat, especially if puréed in a food processor, it's very rare for a cat to eat a prekilled carcass. Cats are not the scavengers that dogs are and will rarely touch a carcass killed by anything other then themselves.

Although this feeding system may work for him, most pet owners I've talked to are not willing to have whole carcasses in their family freezers, don't have that kind of room in their freezers, and aren't willing to feed their dogs that kind of food.

However, if you do have freezer room and are interested in doing this, take some precautions. Make sure the carcasses are cleaned immediately and done so by someone who knows what he or she is doing, so the carcass isn't contaminated by feces. If the carcass isn't to be fed to the dog right away, freeze it with the temperature set at zero degrees Fahrenheit or colder. Thaw the carcass in the refrigerator or give it to the dog frozen; he can gnaw on it.

Watch the dog carefully for problems, including broken teeth, lodged bones, diarrhea, or any other signs of distress, especially while the dog is getting used to this feeding regime.

Commercial Raw Foods

If you would like to feed your pet a raw-food diet but aren't happy about the yuck factor of handling raw meats, there are some commercially prepared raw frozen foods. More and more pet stores are carrying these foods as the demand for them increases.

One risk of these foods is that if they are not handled correctly, even during transportation from the plant to the distributors to the store, when you bring it home, the potential for bacterial contamination is high. These foods must remain frozen.

Read the labels carefully before feeding, so that you feed your pet correctly, and again, handle the food the way it should be handled. Keep in mind, too, that these foods may be frozen, but they are raw foods, so take precautions. Wash your hands, and wash the countertops and the food bowls.

An Excellent Frozen Raw Dog Food
....

Dr. Billinghurst is known as the father of the raw-food movement. His BARF Combo is an excellent commercial raw food. (BARF stands for Bones and Raw Foods.) The BARF Combo contains beef, lamb, chicken, pork, finely ground beef, lamb, pork and chicken bones, beef liver, beef kidney, whole egg without shell, cultured kefir, carrot, broccoli, spinach, bok choy, celery, ground flaxseed, dried alfalfa meal, unbleached beef tripe, apple, pear, grapefruit, orange, dried kelp powder, cod liver oil, capsicum, garlic, vitamin E supplement, zinc oxide, and manganese oxide. Protein is no less than 13.5 percent; fat is no less than 11 percent; fiber is no more than 5 percent; and moisture is no more than 68 percent. *www.barfproducts.com.*

Recipes for Dogs

Transitional Recipe: Beef and Broccoli.............

This recipe is eaten quite readily, especially by dogs who have never before eaten a raw-food diet. This can be fed as a meal or as an addition to a commercial food while progressing toward a raw-food diet. If fed as a complete meal, this recipe is about 1,200 calories, or one day's worth, for an average forty- to fifty-pound dog.

(Note: The vegetables are lightly steamed so the dog can more easily digest them.)

2 cups beef, raw, ground, or muscle meat chopped into
    bite-sized pieces
1 egg, chicken, large, uncooked
$^1/_4$ cup carrots, grated finely, lightly steamed
$^1/_4$ cup broccoli florets, chopped, lightly steamed
1 tablespoon flaxseed meal
$^1/_2$ cup yogurt, regular, plain

1. Mix the first five ingredients together in a bowl, mixing thoroughly, like you're making a meatloaf.
2. Once mixed, if you're adding any supplements, add them now and mix again.
3. Divide the meat into servings. If you're adding to a commercial food, give a fifty-pound dog one meatball-sized piece. If fed as a complete meal, divide in half and feed one-half in the morning and one-half in the evening.
4. Add a portion of the yogurt when you serve the food.

Refrigerate remaining food in an airtight container. It will be good in the refrigerator for one to two days; freeze excess.

Suggested supplements (see chapter 6) include the following:

- a good-quality natural vitamin and mineral supplement
- a fatty acid supplement, such as chicken fat, cod liver oil, salmon oil, fish oil, or safflower oil
- a bonemeal supplement: either natural bonemeal, finely ground eggshells, or a calcium lactate supplement
- a green-food supplement, such as blue-green algae, spirulina, or barley grass
- a health food blend, such as Springtime, Inc.'s Longevity or Tri-Natural Product's Missing Link

Supplements should be added as the food is served.

Variations (using the same amounts as for the original ingredients):

- Use bison instead of beef.
- Use fresh spinach instead of broccoli.

Reba's Rabbit Favorite . . . .

Reba, an Irish setter, was rescued from a neglectful home, where she was fed cheap commercial dog food. This is Reba's favorite recipe and contains about 1,200 calories, one day's meals for the average forty- to fifty-pound dog. Her new owner says that on this diet her once-thin coat has now grown out and is a luxurious, bright red.

3 cups rabbit, ground or muscle meat
1 cup spinach, fresh
1/2 cup yam, fresh
2 tablespoons cod liver oil
1 tablespoon flaxseed meal
1 tablespoon molasses
1 cup yogurt, plain, regular

1. Cut the rabbit meat into small, bite-sized pieces and set aside.
2. Cut the spinach into small pieces, and place on a microwave-safe plate. Add the yam, also cut into small pieces. Cover with a wet paper towel and steam in the microwave, low heat, for about thirty seconds.
3. Add the spinach and yam to the meat. Add the cod liver oil, molasses, and flaxseed meal and stir well, making sure

the ingredients are well mixed so the dog can't leave the greens behind.

4. Divide into two meals. Add half of the yogurt to each meal when serving.

Refrigerate unused portion. Food will remain good in the refrigerator for a day or two; freeze unused meals.

Suggested supplements include the following:

- a good-quality natural vitamin and mineral supplement
- a bonemeal supplement; either natural bonemeal, finely ground eggshells, or a calcium lactate supplement
- a green-food supplement, such as blue-green algae, spirulina, or barley grass
- a health food blend, such as Springtime, Inc.'s Longevity or Tri-Natural Product's Missing Link

Supplements should be added as the food is served.

Variations (using the same amounts as for the original ingredients):

- Use other greens (romaine, swiss chard, collard, kale, turnip, dandelion) in place of the spinach.
- Use sweet potato in place of the yam.
- Use honey instead of the molasses.
- Use kefir instead of yogurt.

Venison and Greens . . . .

This raw food recipe produces about 1,200 calories, good for a fifty-pound dog of average activity.

3 cups venison, raw, ground or muscle meat
1/4 cup spinach, fresh
1/4 cup broccoli florets, fresh
1/4 cup romaine lettuce, fresh
1/4 cup barley grass or wheat grass, fresh
1/2 cup sweet potato, fresh
2 tablespoons cod liver oil
1 tablespoon flaxseed meal
1 tablespoon molasses
1 cup yogurt, plain, regular

1. Cut the venison meat into small, bite-sized pieces and set aside.
2. Cut all the greens into small pieces and place on a microwave safe plate. Cover with a wet paper towel and steam in the microwave, low heat, for about thirty seconds.
3. Steam the sweet potato until soft.
4. Add the greens and sweet potato to the meat. Add the cod liver oil, molasses, and flaxseed meal and stir well, making sure the ingredients are well mixed so the dog can't leave the greens behind.
5. Divide into two meals. Add half of the yogurt to each meal when serving.

Refrigerate unused portion. Food will remain good in the refrigerator for a day or two; freeze unused meals.

Suggested supplements include the following:

- a good-quality natural vitamin and mineral supplement
- a bonemeal supplement: either natural bonemeal, finely ground eggshells, or a calcium lactate supplement

- a green-food supplement, such as blue-green algae, spirulina, or barley grass.
- a health food blend, such as Springtime, Inc.'s Longevity or Tri-Natural Product's Missing Link.

Supplements should be added as the food is served.

Variations (using the same amounts as for the original ingredients):

- Use honey instead of the molasses.
- Use kefir instead of yogurt.

Give Your Dog a Bone. . . . .

Every dog deserves a treat once in a while; here's a really good one.

> 1 large beef knucklebone, raw, with some attached
> marrow bone
> 1 teaspoon cod liver oil
> 1 tablespoon flaxseed meal
> 1 dash garlic powder

1. Using a narrow knife, scrape all of the marrow out of the bone and put it in a small bowl.
2. Add the last three ingredients to the marrow and mix well.
3. Using a spoon and the narrow knife, put the mixture back into the bone. Smear any leftovers all over the knuckle (joint) part of the bone.

Give the bone to your dog and sit back to watch him enjoy it. If your dog is a power chewer and breaks off any long splinters of bone, take those away; don't let him swallow those.

Recipes for Cats

Transitional Recipe: Tigger's Oyster Delight . . . .

Tigger is a big gray and black tabby cat who began begging for oysters when his owner served them to guests. His owner formulated this recipe and says Tigger always enjoys it. (Make sure you buy the raw oysters and tuna from a reputable source, as raw seafood can easily become contaminated.) This can be fed as a meal or as an addition to a commercial food while progressing toward a raw food diet. This recipe is about 350 calories, or one day's supply for a ten-pound indoor cat.

1 cup oysters, raw
$1/4$ cup tuna, raw, cut into fine pieces
1 egg, chicken, hard-boiled, shelled, crumbled
1 teaspoon cod liver oil
2 tablespoons carrots, grated
2 tablespoons wheatgrass, finely chopped

1. Put the oysters, tuna, cod liver oil, and egg into a food processor and liquefy until a thick paste. Pour into a bowl.
2. Add the carrots and wheatgrass and stir well.
3. Divide into servings.

Refrigerate in an airtight container. Food will remain good for one to two days. Do not freeze leftovers; discard after two days.

Suggested daily supplements (see chapter 6) include the following:

- a good-quality natural vitamin and mineral supplement

- a 250 to 500 mg taurine supplement, given according to the product's directions
- a bonemeal supplement: either natural bonemeal, finely ground eggshells, or a calcium lactate supplement
- a green-food supplement, such as blue-green algae, spirulina, or barley grass
- A health food blend, such as Tri-Natural Products Missing Link for Cats

Supplements should be added as the food is served.

Turkey and Squash ....

This is a fairly simple recipe that most cats enjoy. It can be added to a commercial diet to help the cat transition to raw foods. It can also be fed as a daily diet and supplies a ten-pound indoor cat with about 350 calories.

1 cup turkey meat, raw
$^1/_4$ chicken neck, raw
$^1/_4$ cup squash, summer, grated,
   slightly steamed
1 tablespoon cod liver oil

1. Chop the chicken neck into quarters, bones and all. Freeze three pieces for future use and retain one piece for this recipe.
2. Put the chicken neck, turkey meat, grated squash, and cod liver oil into a food processor and liquefy until all ingredients are a thick paste. Add a small amount of water if needed for processing.

3. Add a teaspoon to each of the cat's meals at first, and then over a week or so, gradually increase it to one tablespoon. If fed as a daily diet, divide into meals, store in an airtight container, and refrigerate.
4. Add any supplements when you serve the food.

Food will remain good in the refrigerator for one to two days; freeze excess.

Suggested daily supplements (see chapter 6) include the following:

- a good-quality natural vitamin and mineral supplement
- a 250 to 500 mg taurine supplement, given according to the product's directions
- a bonemeal supplement: either natural bonemeal, finely ground eggshells, or a calcium lactate supplement
- a green-food supplement, such as blue-green algae, spirulina, or barley grass
- a health food blend, such as Tri-Natural Products Missing Link for Cats

Supplements should be added as the food is served.

Variations (using the same amounts as for the original ingredients):

- Use chicken instead of turkey.
- Use another kind of squash rather than summer squash.
- Use grated zucchini instead of squash.

CHAPTER SIX

All You Need to Know about Supplements

Supplements derived from foods can be an excellent source of added nutrients for your dog or cat. They can help address specific conditions your pet may be facing, or they can serve to prevent potential problems.

Most important, though, for most dogs and cats, supplements can fill in the gaps of a nutritional program. As we've seen, commercial foods vary in quality from horrible to excellent, as do many homemade foods, raw or cooked. In addition, the quality of ingredients in any of these diets can very tremendously. Wisely chosen and used supplements can help balance those foods so that your dog or cat is well nourished.

The Basics of Supplements

A supplement is anything that is added to a diet or food formula. It can be a whole food (such as yogurt or kefir); it can be a mixture of ingredients (such as Tri-Natural's Missing Link, see pages 125 and 130); or it may be an herb in a capsule or tea.

Supplements should be chosen with care, both for their ingredients and for their quality. An herbal remedy called ginseng, for example, could be one of three different plants. The Asian or Korean ginseng (panax ginseng) is the original medicinal ginseng. American ginseng (panax quinquefolius) is a close relative with similar properties. Siberian ginseng, however, is a different plant altogether (eleutherococcus senticosus). To be safe, make sure you use products from known companies who have a good reputation.

The supplement should also be of a reasonable price. Once you begin giving this to your pet, you want to be able to continue. If a supplement is too expensive, you may not be able to afford to keep giving it to your pet, even should your pet show favorable reactions to it. Now, granted, often the better-quality supplements do cost more because they have higher-quality ingredients. But sometimes a company may be trying to recover research costs by boosting the cost of a product, and although this is perfectly legitimate, it may mean you can find the same product somewhere else for less.

You should also be able to give this supplement to your pet without trouble. You don't want to have to coax your cat to eat an unpleasant substance every time you feed him or her; nor do you want to have to shove a pill down your dog's throat every day. If a supplement is difficult to give, you're not going to do it as often as you should. A supplement made to taste good to dogs or cats is best so the pet eats it willingly.

The supplement should also accomplish something. Yogurt adds beneficial bacteria to the animal's digestive system and adds protein and other nutrients to the pet's diet, for example. These accomplishments are tough to see, but if your dog or cat is digest-

> ### A Whole Food Supplement for Dogs
> ....
> Missing Link Supplement for Dogs is made from whole foods and is designed to fill the nutritional gaps that might be present in a dog's diet. Ingredients include flaxseed, blackstrap molasses, rice bran, primary dried yeast, sunflower seeds, freeze-dried liver, alfalfa, carrot, freeze-dried bone, fish meal, oyster, sprouted green barley, kelp, lecithin, garlic, and yucca extract. Protein is not less than 18 percent; fat not less than 28 percent; fiber not less than 10 percent; moisture not more than 10 percent. There are 40 calories per tablespoon. www.trinatural.com.

ing food well, the stools look good, the eyes are bright, and the coat is shiny, well, things are going well. However, if you're adding a supplement for another reason, say perhaps to help your pet's stiffness in the morning, and you're not seeing any changes after a couple of months, it's probably time to try something else.

Unpleasant side effects are common with many medications, but daily supplements should not cause any. Diarrhea is common in some dogs when their diet is changed in any way, and for these dogs supplements should be changed gradually. Some supplements will change the stool color. Blue-green algae supplements will cause the stools to be darker than normal, sometimes even a dark blue-green color, but this is fine and causes no problems for the dog or cat. However, there should be no negative side effects such as flatulence (gas), diarrhea, or vomiting.

Vitamins and Minerals

In chapter 2 we discussed what vitamins and minerals are and what part they play in your pet's nutrition. We also listed some foods where those could be found. Ideally, your pet should receive all the vitamins and minerals he needs from the foods he eats. Unfortunately, as we've said previously, without sending all your pet's individual foods out for a nutritional analysis, it's impossible to make sure that happens. However, a vitamin and mineral supplement can help fill in any vitamin and mineral gaps in your pet's diet.

Many vitamins and mineral supplements will use synthetic sources; if there is a list of chemical names in the ingredients list rather than whole foods, these are synthetic vitamins and minerals. The best vitamin and mineral supplements are those made from whole foods rather than chemically processed formulations. Joan Weiskopf, a veterinary clinical nutritionist and author of *Pet Food Nation* (Harper Collins, 2007), says, "Whole food nutrients are by and large the most usable (bioavailable) and bioactive in the body."

In addition, many pets may balk at eating strange foods. If your dog has eaten dry kibble foods all his or her life, when you put cooked or raw meat in front of him, he'll probably eat it. He may even try to gulp it! But when you offer him some grated carrots, chopped spinach, and cooked squash, he may refuse to eat it. His thought is, "That's not dog food!" (And this is why so many of my recipes ask for the meat to be chopped or ground and the other ingredients well mixed in; it's harder for your dog to pick and choose this way.) Cats can be even more finicky. So you may be providing all the right foods, but that's no guarantee your pet will eat them all.

Kerry Brown, DVM, a holistic practitioner, recommends a daily supplement of a vitamins and minerals. Shawn Messonnier, DVM, agrees: "Every pet can benefit from a good natural vitamin-mineral supplement. No diet is perfect and using this supplement assures us that the pet has at least obtained the essential macro and micronutrients each day." He recommends a raw, natural human supplement, although he suggests following your veterinarian's guidance for dosages if you do. No matter what brand you decide to use, the vitamin-mineral supplement should contain all of the essential vitamin and minerals; see chapter 2 for a complete list.

Vitamin B Complex

Wendy Volhard, author of *Holistic Guide for a Healthy Dog* (Howell, 2000), recommends a vitamin B complex supplement twice a day, morning and evening, with each meal. She says, "Vitamin B complex is made up of 17 individual parts and is flushed through the system quickly; it cannot be stored in the body." The B complex vitamins are important for many body processes, including healing. This advice applies to cats as well as dogs.

Although the B complex vitamins are present in many foods, including molasses, yogurt, kefir, and eggs, they are also easily destroyed by the heat of food cooking and processing. A supplement can help prevent deficiencies.

Vitamin C

Dr. Goldstein also recommends a vitamin C supplement for both dogs and cats: "Vitamin C is involved in many metabolic and physiological processes of the body. While animals do manufacture vitamin C, the body's reserves are quickly used up in high free radical production situations, such as the ingestion of chemical additives and preservatives, exposure to insecticides, herbicides, and environmental pollutants."

There are several forms of vitamin C, including ascorbic acid and calcium ascorbate. Ascorbic acid is the antioxidant part of vitamin C. It is tart and most dogs won't eat it; cats won't touch it. Calcium ascorbate is more easily absorbed by the intestinal tract. It can be mixed with meat, yogurt, or eggs, and most animals will readily eat it.

Calcium-Phosphorus

Calcium and phosphorus have many functions in the body, individually and together, but one of the most important is the growth and maintenance of healthy bones and teeth. The balance of calcium to phosphorus is very important, as a deficiency of either can affect both.

When feeding a homemade diet, either a partial one added to commercial pet foods, or a complete home-cooked or raw diet, the balance of calcium to phosphorus is easily upset. Meats are high in phosphorus and low in calcium; bones are high in calcium and low in phosphorus. The ideal ratio is 1.3 parts calcium to 1 part phosphorus. If a diet is high in meat, this ration can be achieved by adding some bones to the diet or by offering a natural bonemeal supplement. Dr. Messonnier recommends using natural bonemeal or bonemeal tablets for both cats and dogs.

Zinc

This often-forgotten mineral is important for many bodily functions, including a healthy immune system. Poor-quality commercial dog and cat foods, especially the generic brands, have been known to cause zinc deficiencies.

Antioxidants

Antioxidants function in the body as scavengers for free radicals. Free radicals are the by-product of oxidation and can create havoc in the body. Common antioxidants include vitamins A, C, and E, as well as the minerals selenium, manganese, and zinc. Some food additives have antioxidants, also, including gingko biloba.

Taurine

Taurine is an amino acid that is found in meats, poultry, eggs, dairy products, and fish. This is an amino acid that dogs produce internally in sufficient quantities, and although cats do not produce taurine themselves, they require it daily and so must obtain it from their diet. Unfortunately, taurine deficiencies can produce blindness and heart failure.

Cats eating a homemade diet, even a raw one with plenty of meat, should receive a taurine supplement to make sure they have adequate levels. A therapeutic dose is 250 to 500 mg daily.

Food Supplements

My mother was one of those moms who would heat up the chicken soup as soon as anyone sniffled, said they didn't feel good, or became warm to the touch. She also made us drink orange juice when we had a cold, or even when exposed to someone else who had a cold. Before the advent of modern medicine, foods and herbal remedies were the basis of the

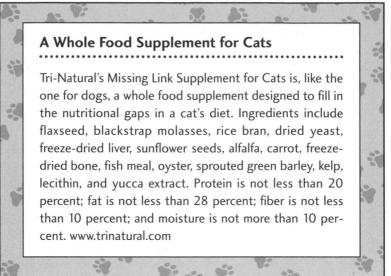

A Whole Food Supplement for Cats

Tri-Natural's Missing Link Supplement for Cats is, like the one for dogs, a whole food supplement designed to fill in the nutritional gaps in a cat's diet. Ingredients include flaxseed, blackstrap molasses, rice bran, dried yeast, freeze-dried liver, sunflower seeds, alfalfa, carrot, freeze-dried bone, fish meal, oyster, sprouted green barley, kelp, lecithin, and yucca extract. Protein is not less than 20 percent; fat is not less than 28 percent; fiber is not less than 10 percent; and moisture is not more than 10 percent. www.trinatural.com

medicines used for people and their domestic animals. We'll discuss herbal remedies later in this chapter, but let's take a look at foods that have both good nutrition and the potential for helping prevent problems.

These foods can be used as ingredients in your pet's food, and as you look through the recipes in this book, you'll find that many of the recipes already contain many of them. You can also add some of these foods as a supplement to boost your pet's nutrition. Molasses, for example, is high in many minerals and some of the B complex vitamins. Although cats don't taste sugar, dogs enjoy the taste, and it can make other foods, like vitamin C, more palatable.

- **Alfalfa.** This is a very nutritious plant, and even when dried contains proteins, vitamins, minerals, and phyto-

nutrients. It is thought to have cancer-fighting properties and is good for the pet's mental health.

- **Apple.** Apples are good for healthy skin and are good for
the liver.
- **Apple cider vinegar.** Apple cider vinegar is high in
many minerals. It also has antibacterial qualities and is
known to boost the immune system.
- **Bee pollen.** This contains a number of enzymes, antioxidants, and other essential nutrients.
- **Bilberry.** This fruit is related to the blueberry and is
known to help with disorders of the eyes. It is also helpful for the circulatory system.
- **Blue-green algae.** Spirulina is a blue-green, freshwater
algae. It is an antioxidant, a good source of B complex
vitamins, many minerals, and is considered a powerful
phytonutrient.
- **Bonemeal.** Bonemeal is a good source of calcium and
when added to a home-cooked or raw-food diet, will balance the phosphorus that is present in meat.
- **Bromelain.** Pineapple and pineapple juice contain
bromelain, a digestive enzyme that can assist the body in
digesting and metabolizing foods. It also has mild anti-
inflammatory properties.
- **Capsaicin.** Capsaicin is the portion of peppers that makes
them taste hot. It increases blood flow by dilating blood
vessels and has been used in cats with cardiomyopathy.
- **Carrot.** Carrots are high in antioxidants and vitamins
A, C, and E. They are high in enzymes and minerals.
- **Chondroitin.** Chondroitin is found in animal cartilage
and helps inhibit the enzymes that are destructive to
joint tissue. It is most often used in conjunction with
glucosamine.

- **Cod liver oil.** Did your grandmother try to get you to eat a tablespoon of cod liver oil every day? Mine did, and she had good reason: this is a rich source of the fat-soluble vitamins A and D, plus it's a rich source of essential fatty acids.
- **Cranberry.** Cranberries (and cranberry juice) have been used to prevent bladder and urinary tract disorders (in people, dogs, and cats) for many years. Rather than creating a more acidic environment in the bladder, as was previously thought, cranberry works by preventing bacteria from adhering to the bladder and urinary tract walls.
- **Dandelion.** This green contains many minerals, vitamins, and phytonutrients. It is helpful for the liver's function and healing and is a mild diuretic.
- **Eggs.** Eggs are a complete source of protein, containing all of the essential amino acids. They are also rich in B complex vitamins, minerals, and vitamins A and E. The shells are excellent sources of calcium.
- **Fish oil.** Fish oils contain the all important omega-3 fatty acids.
- **Flaxseed oil.** This is a high-quality oil containing both omega-3 and omega-6 fatty acids. It should be used in very small amounts, as it can cause diarrhea in some dogs and cats. (Flaxseed meal is not as concentrated as the oil and does not cause diarrhea. This can be used instead.)
- **Green foods.** *Green foods* is an umbrella term for many dark green plant foods that are nutritious with medicinal properties. The term usually includes barley grass (rich in vitamins and minerals), spirulina (a powerful phyto-

nutrient), alfalfa (a very nutritious food), and chlorophyll (rich in anti-inflammatories).

- **Honey.** Honey is a nutritious additive for foods and can be used in dog and cat foods for its nutritional benefits. Cats will eat it even though they do not have the taste receptors for sugar. Honey is high in carbohydrates, minerals, and B complex vitamins.
- **Kefir.** Kefir is a cultivated, enzyme-rich food filled with friendly microorganisms that is generally more nutritious than yogurt. Made from grains, it is known to stimulate the digestive enzymes, thereby making the entire digestive tract more efficient. It is also more easily digested than yogurt.
- **Kelp.** Kelp is a seaweed, and when dried it is an excellent source of iodine. It is also rich in minerals and vitamins.
- **Molasses.** Molasses is high in potassium and contains several B complex vitamins.
- **Nutritional yeast.** Nutritional yeast is grown on molasses and is a nonactive yeast (it doesn't raise bread). It is full of B vitamins, protein, trace minerals, and salt.
- **Reishi mushroom.** This is particularly effective for kittens suffering from upper respiratory disease and both dogs and cats suffering from bronchial disease. It is also a known immune system stimulant.
- **Safflower oil.** Safflower oil contains all of the essential fatty acids. It is highly palatable, and almost all dogs and cats will readily eat it.
- **Yogurt.** Yogurt that has "live active cultures" on its label, is a good source for the beneficial bacteria needed by the intestinal tract for optimal digestion. The bacteria is lactobacillus acidophilus. Yogurt also contains proteins and fats.

Herbal Supplements

Herbal remedies (or herbal medicinals) are plants known or thought to have medicinal or nutritional benefits for people and animals. Plants have been used as medicine for as long as we know. Plants were used as medicine by the Native Americans and ancient Europeans. They were even used as far back as five thousand years in ancient China.

The recent resurgence in these traditional remedies has come about because many people are concerned about the side effects that modern drugs have; sometimes the side effects seem worse than the original problem that is being treated. Many people are also looking for more natural approaches to health care, and this encompasses both nutrition and medicine.

Herbal remedies are still the primary medicine for people all around the world. The World Health Organization (WHO) states that 80 percent of the world's population uses herbal remedies or medicines as a part of their regular health care.

Some of the herbal remedies commonly used with domestic pets, eaten as a food or ingested with food or water, include:

- **Chamomile.** This herb is very calming to the digestive tract and has been useful for car sickness in pets. It has also been used for inflammatory bowel disease.
- **Echinacea.** This herb strengthens the immune system and has antiviral and antibacterial properties. It also helps the body heal more quickly after illnesses.
- **Ginger.** Ginger is useful for upset stomachs; a ginger cookie or tea can help prevent car sickness.
- **Gingko biloba.** Gingko biloba has been shown to be effective for some older pets with cognitive dysfunction. It has also been used for kidney disease and incontinence.

- **Ginseng.** This herb has been used by the owners of performance dogs, as it decreases glycogen use in muscles, thereby reducing fatigue. It has also been used as a treatment for diabetes, and it's known for stimulating the immune system.
- **Goldenrod.** This herb increases the flow of urine, washing out bacteria and small stones. It also calms spasms in the urinary tract.
- **Goldenseal.** This is an effective antibacterial for the digestive tract.
- **Hawthorn berry.** These berries support the heart and improve the heart's muscle tone.
- **Licorice root.** This is a natural anti-inflammatory; it also supports the liver.
- **Milk thistle.** This herb supports the liver, both its functioning and its healing. It is a strong antioxidant.
- **Mullein.** This helps the respiratory tract and opens airways.
- **Peppermint.** This herb is particularly effective for calming an upset stomach or overactive digestive tract. Peppermint can also be used for car sickness.
- **Red clover.** This herb has been used for centuries as a mild diuretic and a blood cleanser. It is also used to support the liver.
- **Valerian.** This herb calms and soothes and is good for anxiety and fear.
- **Yucca.** This is very beneficial to dogs and cats suffering from arthritis.

Before adding any of these herbal supplements to your pet's diet, contact a local holistic veterinarian. Dosages will vary depending upon the formulation and maker of the herb, as well as the animal and its state of health, size, and weight.

A Whole Food Formula Supplement for Dogs

Springtime, Inc.'s whole food formula supplement for dogs, Longevity, is based on the super phytronutrient, spirulina, a blue-green algae. Other ingredients include bee pollen, beef or pork liver, yeast, chondroitin sulfate, glucosamine, ascorbic acids, citrus bioflavonoids, kelp, sea salts, and biotin. Protein is no less than 33.9 percent; fat is no less than 4.5 percent; fiber is no more than 2.3 percent; and moisture is no more than 7.8 percent.

What Does Your Pet Need?

Determining what supplements your pet needs can be difficult. Dr. Jacobs says, "It is critical to ensure that you're feeding a balanced diet when considering vitamins and minerals. More is not always better, and in fact, can create serious medical problems."

When feeding a homemade diet, the ingredients should provide the majority of vitamins, minerals, essential fatty acids, and other nutrients. However, to boost the foods' benefits and to prevent nutritional deficiencies, you can add the following for adult dogs:

- a good-quality, natural vitamin and mineral supplement
- if the recipe doesn't already contain some oils, a fatty acid supplement, such as chicken fat, cod liver oil, salmon oil, fish oil, or safflower oil

- a bonemeal supplement: either natural bonemeal, finely ground eggshells, or a calcium lactate supplement
- a green-food supplement, such as blue-green algae, spirulina, or barley grass
- a health food blend, such as Springtime, Inc.'s Longevity or Tri-Natural Product's Missing Link

The dosages will vary depending upon your dog's size, weight, age, and state of health. In addition, each supplement maker will have different directions and dosages. Make sure you read the directions.

Cats can have the same supplements, in smaller dosages, but should also have a daily supplement of taurine:

- a good-quality natural vitamin and mineral supplement
- a 250 to 500 mg taurine supplement, given according to the product's directions
- if the recipe doesn't already contain some oils, a fatty acid supplement, such as chicken fat, cod liver oil, salmon oil, fish oil, or safflower oil
- a bonemeal supplement: either natural bonemeal, finely ground eggshells, or a calcium lactate supplement
- a green-food supplement, such as blue-green algae, spirulina, or barley grass
- a health food blend, such as Tri-Natural Products Missing Link for Cats

The most important thing with supplements is to watch your dog or cat. Make sure your pet's health is good; the eyes are bright, the coat shiny, and a good weight maintained. Your pet should have energy for play and work and a good mental outlook.

CHAPTER SEVEN

As You Begin
Making Changes

Making changes to your pet's diet can be distressing, no matter whether you are changing a commercial food, adding new supplements, or if you have decided to create a homemade diet. You'll have doubts: "What if I am doing this incorrectly? Will my dog get sick?" or "What if my kitten won't eat this new food?" Doubts are normal; this is something very new to you and your pet, but you can use those doubts to make sure you think things through prior to making any big changes. But, at the same time, don't let those doubts stop you, either. You can do this, and your pet will appreciate it.

Make Changes Gradually

If your dog or cat has been eating commercial pet foods, it's a good idea to make changes very slowly. Use one of the recipes in chapter 4 that are designed to be added to commercial foods. Chicken and Carrots with Dog Food and Sumptuous Sardines with Cat Food are both easy to prepare and serve. You can begin by adding just a tablespoonful for dogs and a teaspoonful for cats to their normal commercial food.

Watch for upset tummies (anxiety, lack of appetite, vomiting) or poor stools (soft or liquid), as these can be signs your pet is suffering from some gastrointestinal upset. If he or she is, offer a little yogurt or kefir, and decrease the new food slightly. Wait until things settle down, and then very slowly begin offering the new food again. Make sure you give your pet's system plenty of time to adjust; these are very new foods.

Introducing Home-Cooked Recipes

If you want to eventually transfer your pet over to a completely home-cooked diet, you can begin by adding some of the new recipes to your pet's commercial food, as explained above, and then gradually decrease the old food and increase the new, as was explained in chapter 4. The change may need to be stretched out over several weeks and sometimes even over a few months. Take as much time as your pet needs so that he or she can become accustomed to it.

As you try new recipes or add new ingredients, again, do so gradually. You should end up with four or five recipes plus a few variations of each. This will make sure your pet is being fed a variety of ingredients, both meats and other proteins, as well as some plant products. Although your dog or cat may initially be hesitant to try new foods, as he gets used to this new feeding regime, he'll be more open to change. In addition, his digestive tract will also become used to new foods.

Introducing Dogs to Raw Foods

Introducing a pet to a raw-food diet may take time, too, because it's so different. It's usually a lot of fun, though, because of your pet's reactions to it. Many dogs will look at a chunk of meat, sniff it, and then look at their owners with amazement, "I can have this? Really?" Then some, perhaps afraid that their owner may change his or her mind, will try to gulp it and swallow it whole! That's why most of the raw-food recipes in this book recommend cutting the meat into bite-sized pieces. Although tearing the meat off the bone is normal behavior and good for the dog's teeth and jaws, and many raw food enthusiasts say to feed the dog chunks of meat and bones, I feel the dog has to get past the overstimulation and excitement phase where he might actually choke himself.

I've also talked to the owners of a few dogs who refuse to touch a raw-food recipe; most of the owners seem to feel that the foods were just too different and their dogs were cautious about unknown things. If the recipes are introduced very gradually, however, and mixed in with the foods the dog is used to eating, most will eventually accept it.

Dealing with Cats and Change

Cats can be incredibly finicky and may refuse new foods altogether, to the point of going hungry. If your cat is reluctant to try new foods, you may want to try what I did with Havoc, my oldest cat. Havoc grew up eating dry kibble cat foods. When I began trying new recipes, all of my other cats would at least sniff and taste the new foods, but not Havoc. It took me three years to wean him off dry cat foods!

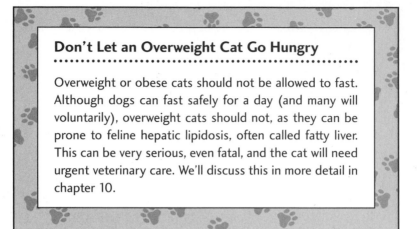

Don't Let an Overweight Cat Go Hungry

Overweight or obese cats should not be allowed to fast. Although dogs can fast safely for a day (and many will voluntarily), overweight cats should not, as they can be prone to feline hepatic lipidosis, often called fatty liver. This can be very serious, even fatal, and the cat will need urgent veterinary care. We'll discuss this in more detail in chapter 10.

Just make sure that you introduce the new recipes, cooked or raw, very gradually. With Havoc, I began offering the foods as treats, and I used jealousy between him and my other cats as incentive for him. The other cats were getting treats, praise, and time with my husband and I. Finally, the jealousy won out, and he wanted to be a part of the fun. When he would try a new food, I would give him petting and praise, even if he spit it back out. At least he tried it. Eventually he discovered a few foods he liked.

First Steps

So, you want to change your pet's diet. What's the first step? Let's take a look at your kitchen first. You are going to need a few tools; you may already have them, but let's make sure. Some may be hidden in the far reaches of a cupboard.

- **Grater.** A hand grater is fine; it just needs to be sharp so you can grate carrots, zucchini, and some other fresh vegetables.
- **Sharp knives.** You'll need a knife for chopping vegetables and a knife for cutting meats. If you also want to offer your pets some raw bones, you may need a knife that can cut through joints or chicken necks.
- **Cutting board.** A wooden cutting board is fine. (You need to be able to easily disinfect it after you have had raw meat on it.)
- **Food processor or blender.** This should be powerful enough to liquefy meats and strong enough to grind up eggshells. A strong blender or food processor is well worth the money you spend on it.
- **Meat grinder.** If you want to grind up bones to add natural bonemeal to your pet's food, you'll need a meat grinder. If you don't have one, your butcher may be able to do this for you.
- **Food storage containers.** You will need containers to store food in the refrigerator and freezer, and they should be marked as pet food so family members don't try to eat these foods for dinner.

You will also need a few bowls of various sizes, mixing spoons, a microwave plate or two, and some other commonly used kitchen items.

Some Common Pet-Food Ingredients

Listed below are some common pet-food ingredients; however, don't go shopping and buy all of these. In the beginning of this chapter I said, "Make changes gradually," and I mean it. Choose a few recipes that sound good to you, and begin making just those recipes at first. Then you can try some new things.

You can, however, use this list as a resource when you try new recipes or when you're choosing foods at the grocery store or farmer's market.

- **Meats.** Beef, bison, venison, elk, rabbit, chicken, duck, turkey, and goose. The cuts are not important, as long as it's muscle meat. You may also want to feed your pet some organ meats, such as hearts and livers.
- **Fish.** Just about any deboned fish, including trout, bass, catfish, salmon, tuna, mackerel, or herring, as well as clams and oysters. Lobster, if you want to share.
- **Dairy and eggs.** Goat's milk (no cow's milk), fresh and aged cheeses (including goat cheese and cottage cheese), yogurt, chicken eggs, duck eggs, quail eggs, and goose eggs.
- **Vegetables.** Carrots, spinach, broccoli, zucchini, squash of all kinds, pumpkin, green beans, kidney beans, sweet potatoes, yams, and potatoes.
- **Fruits.** Apples (no seeds), bananas, pears, and watermelon.
- **Cereal grains.** Barley, oatmeal, wild or brown rice, flaxseeds, and millet.
- **Other good foods.** Kefir is good nutrition and great for the digestion. Fish oils, safflower oil, sesame seed oil, or olive oil for some taste and fat content. Cats love salmon oil. Use tomatoes sparingly; they are nutritious, but the acid content can be tough on some digestive tracts.

When you go shopping, choose foods of good quality, foods you would be comfortable feeding your family.

Feeding Time

Feeding your dog or cat should be calm and peaceful. Don't put the bowl in the middle of the kitchen and expect your pet to eat in peace while you're cooking dinner, the kids are coming in to get the dishes and silverware to set the table for dinner, and Dad is coming in for a soda. That's much too hectic—and why some dogs begin to protect their food and why some cats will leave their food uneaten.

Feed your dogs or cats in a safe place where no one will bother them while they're eating. For dogs, it can even be in their crates, if they're crate trained. Cats often like to eat in an elevated location; the ledge on a cat tree is great.

No Free Feeding

Free feeding is the practice of putting food down and leaving it all day. If your pet is being switched over to a home-cooked or raw diet, it's especially important not to free feed. With home-cooked or raw foods, spoilage is a huge issue if the food is left out all the time.

Your dog will need set meal times. You can feed your dog two meals, morning and evening, or if your dog prefers, just feed him once per day. It's really up to you and your dog. But whatever you decide, set the meal down, and then set the kitchen timer for twenty minutes. If your dog has walked away from the bowl when the timer goes off, pick up the bowl; the meal's over. (If he's still eating, obviously let him finish.)

Don't offer anything else until the next scheduled meal; if he begs, too bad. It only takes two or three incomplete meals before most dogs figure out the new regime.

Cats, now, often eat more often than twice a day. You may need to set up three or four feeding times. Perhaps once in the morning before you go to work, one when you first get home in the evening, and then another meal before you go to bed.

Multiple Advantages

When a dog or cat is provided with food all the time, as with free feeding, the food is always available, and your pet tends to pick at the food. If there should ever be a health scare, the first questions your vet will ask are, "How is his appetite? Did he eat his last meal all right? How much did he eat?" You won't be able to answer.

In addition, house-training a puppy or a kitten is significantly easier if the baby is on a set feeding schedule. When he eats at specific times, he will need to move his bowels on a regular schedule, too. You can then get the puppy outside or the kitten to the litter box.

And last, but not least, when you provide your dog or cat with meals, set meals at scheduled times. You are the giver of the food, and this just helps strengthen the bond between the two of you.

Dishes and Bowls

Dogs.   I prefer to use stainless steel bowls for my dogs. The stainless steel bowls are tough, won't break even if the dog picks them up and drops them, and are easy to clean. They aren't cheap, but they will also last for a dog's lifetime.

Large- and giant-breed dogs will appreciate it if their food bowls are elevated slightly; elbow height is great. There are stands made especially for this purpose, or you can set the bowl on a food stool or on the crossbar of a stepladder. Not only does this make eating easier for these dogs, but it helps them swallow. The food can also then proceed more easily down the esophagus to the stomach.

Cats.   I use ceramic saucers or bowls for the cats. You might wish to use plastic, but some cats can develop acne on the chin because bacteria built up in the pores of the plastic. Most cats also dislike deep bowls, so saucers work well. If you're giving your cat a food that is very soupy, then you can use a shallow bowl.

It's very important to wash all of the dishes daily. The ingredients in home-cooked and raw foods can spoil easily if not refrigerated, and even those pets who lick their dishes clean can leave microscopic bits of food that can go bad.

Food Portions

Deciding how much food your dog or cat needs of a home-cooked diet can be difficult. Just as the directions for one particular commercial food may instruct you to feed a fifty-pound dog three full cups of food, and another brand may say to feed him only two cups, your homemade meals will vary. Cat foods vary too.

Although eventually you will be able to judge just by looking at the ingredients of a given recipe, in the beginning you will want to keep track of calories to judge how much food your pet should be fed.

The National Research Council recommends the following for adult dogs of average activity levels:

- A 5-pound dog needs 244 calories per day.
- A 10-pound dog needs 411 calories per day.
- A 20-pound dog needs 691 calories per day.
- A 35-pound dog needs 1,051 calories per day.
- A 50-pound dog needs 1,374 calories per day.
- A 70-pound dog needs 1,768 calories per day.
- A 90-pound dog needs 2,135 calories per day.
- A 100-pound dog needs 2,311 calories per day.
- A 120-pound dog needs 2,649 calories per day.
- A 150-pound dog needs 3,132 calories per day.

The calorie needs of pregnant and nursing dogs as well as puppies are listed in chapter 8. The needs of adult dogs, including active and working dogs, are in chapter 9, and special-needs dogs are in chapter 10.

The recommendations for indoor adult cats are as follows:

- A 4-pound cat needs 127 calories per day.
- A 5-pound cat needs 159 calories per day.
- A 7-pound cat needs 223 calories per day.
- A 9-pound cat needs 286 calories per day.
- An 11-pound cat needs 350 calories per day.

The recommendations for outdoor adult cats are as follows:

- A 4-pound cat needs 145 calories per day.

- A 5-pound cat needs 159 calories per day.
- A 7-pound cat needs 255 calories per day.
- A 9-pound cat needs 327 calories per day.
- An 11-pound cat needs 400 calories per day.

The calorie needs of pregnant and nursing cats as well as kittens are listed in chapter 8, and special-needs cats are in chapter 10.

When Dogs Guard Their Food

Dogs who guard their food, often called resource guarders by behaviorists, often do so because they're afraid it will be taken away from them. Owners can unwittingly make this worse by messing with their dog's food.

The owner of a Labrador retriever told me she had seen a segment on a cable show where shelter workers were testing a dog that was going up for adoption by putting a fake hand in the dog's bowl of food. The dog attacked the hand, failed the test, and had to be euthanized. She didn't want this to happen to her dog, so every day as she fed the dog, she would reach in with her hand and mess with her dog's food. The dog, who had never shown any signs of resource guarding, became so worried about her food that she did begin to guard it.

Let your dog eat in peace. If you, for any reason, feel that your dog may guard his food, call a behaviorist for assistance. Don't try to "fix" this on your own.

Storing the Food

Handle the food you get for your pets as you would your family's food. Refrigerate cooked foods right after cooking; airtight containers work best. Most cooked foods will remain good in the refrigerator for two to three days. If you make a big batch of food for more than three days, freeze the excess.

Raw foods, especially meats, should be refrigerated all the time, even on the drive home from the store if you live more than ten to fifteen minutes away. Just fill a cooler with ice and bring the meat home in the cooler. Most meats will remain fresh for a couple of days in the refrigerator; freeze any meats you need to keep for longer than that.

Thaw frozen meats in the refrigerator; don't thaw them at room temperature. If they thaw completely and warm up too much before you notice, bacteria will proliferate very quickly.

Frozen foods, especially meats, will remain good in the freezer for three to four months. Date the package when you put it in the freezer so you can track how old it is.

Keep a Feeding Journal

When you begin changing your pet's food, keep a journal or make notes on the calendar. At the beginning keep detailed notes about your pet:

- the date
- your pet's weight
- general condition
- skin and coat condition
- mental attitude

- eating habits
- overall health and any medical conditions
- urine and feces and whether there are any problems
- food changes you are instituting now and your eventual goals

Detail in the journal or on the calendar any food changes, recipes tried, and the results, including your dog's or cat's reactions. If there are any foods your pet particularly likes, jot those down, and if there are any he or she dislikes, refuses to eat, or has a bad reaction to, make note of those, too.

At three weeks, six weeks, and twelve weeks, take another look at your pet, making note of everything you noted at the beginning. Reevaluate the diet and decide whether it's accomplishing the goals you set in the beginning. At these times you can decide whether you need to increase recipe portions because your pet has lost weight or failed to gain weight, or you can do the opposite.

You may also want to touch base with your veterinarian at some of these times too. It's important to give your veterinarian the option of deciding how often he or she needs to see your pet, especially if your pet has a health problem.

CHAPTER EIGHT

Feeding Puppies, Kittens, and Their Mothers

Puppies, kittens, and their mothers all have special nutritional needs. Puppies are busy and growing quickly and need good nutrition for healthy growth, especially larger puppies. Kittens, those active little souls, need energy for all that movement. Pregnant and nursing mothers have some very special nutritional requirements so that their babies can develop properly and so that the moms have plenty of milk to nourish the little ones.

Feeding Puppies

Small breeds are considered puppies until about twelve months of age; medium-sized breeds until fourteen to sixteen months of age; and larger breeds until eighteen to twenty months of age.

Puppies need more protein, vitamins and minerals, and calories than do adult dogs. Many times, the recipes for adult dogs can be used for puppies as long as the protein amounts are increased, which will add the needed nutrition. For example, the recipe in chapter 4, Gina's Beef and Cheese, can be converted to a puppy recipe by doubling the eggs in the recipe (from two to four) and the cheese (from a quarter cup to a half cup). The recipe would create then two days' worth of food for a ten-week-old ten-pound puppy or one day's worth of food for a ten-week-old twenty-pound puppy.

How Much?

The calorie recommendations for growing puppies are as follows:

- An eight-week-old five-pound puppy needs 375 calories per day.
- An eight-week-old ten-pound puppy needs 750 calories per day.
- A ten-week-old ten-pound puppy needs 650 calories per day.
- A ten-week-old twenty-pound puppy needs 1,300 calories per day.
- A twelve-week-old, ten-pound puppy needs 560 calories per day.
- A twelve-week-old twenty-pound puppy needs 1,128 calories per day.
- A twelve-week-old, thirty-pound puppy needs 1,680 calories per day.

As you can see, there are many variables as to how many calories growing puppies need. But, as a general rule, a weaned,

rapidly growing puppy will probably need twice as many calories at this stage of life than he will need when he's full grown
and at his adult weight.

When the puppy has reached 40 to 50 percent of his adult
weight, he will need about 1.5 times the calories he will need
as an adult. When he's at 75 to 80 percent of his adult weight,
he will need only about 1.25 times his adult calorie needs.

These are only guidelines, however. Every puppy is an individual. You may find these guidelines suit your puppy wonderfully; or you may discover that your puppy is always hungry and
is not gaining weight, so in that case, increase his calories, proteins, and fats. On the other hand, if your puppy gains too much
weight and is roly-poly, cut back a little. Keep in mind, a lean
(but not skinny) puppy is a healthier puppy than a fat one.

Puppies also grow in spurts; they don't grow consistently
and gradually. When your puppy is getting ready to go through
a growth spurt, he or she may act ravenous—as if there simply
isn't enough food in the world to satisfy his or her hunger. Go
ahead and increase the food a little at a time—too much all at
once will make the puppy sick, until he or she is finished with
that growth spurt.

Commercial Foods

As we discussed in chapter 3, commercial foods vary in quality and that includes puppy foods. Some require the puppy
to eat vast quantities of foods (more than the puppy is able to
eat) to obtain the needed nutrition. Luckily, however, today
there are better foods that can nourish the puppy with quality
ingredients.

Just remember, a commercial food for puppies can be labeled
either a puppy food or for all life stages. Puppy foods tend to be

higher in calories and fat, and many times, in carbohydrates. Just read the labels using the guidelines and tools set out in chapter 3 to choose a food that has the calories your puppy needs, one that is higher in protein and fat and lower in carbohydrates.

Supplement Recommendations

As with all diets, supplements can fill in the nutritional gaps. Since puppies are growing so rapidly and are very active, making sure the puppy has all the necessary nutrition is very important. Deficiencies will show up much more quickly in puppies than they do in adults.

Here are some recommended supplements for puppies:

- a good-quality natural vitamin and mineral supplement
- a fatty acid supplement, such as chicken fat, cod liver oil, salmon oil, fish oil, or safflower oil
- a bonemeal supplement: either natural bonemeal, finely ground eggshells, or a calcium lactate supplement
- a nutritional yeast supplement
- a green-food supplement, such as blue-green algae, spirulina, or barley grass
- a health food blend, such as Springtime, Inc.'s Longevity or Tri-Natural Product's Missing Link

The dosages will vary depending upon your puppy's size, weight, age, and state of health. In addition, each supplement maker will have different directions and dosages. Make sure you read the directions.

Be very careful adding calcium alone to a puppy's diet. Many owners of large- or giant-breed puppies feel that calcium

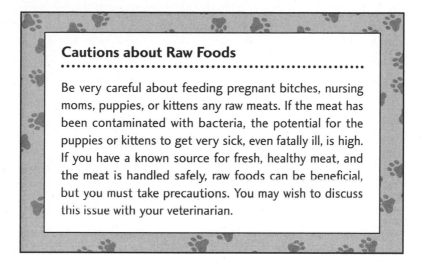

Cautions about Raw Foods

Be very careful about feeding pregnant bitches, nursing moms, puppies, or kittens any raw meats. If the meat has been contaminated with bacteria, the potential for the puppies or kittens to get very sick, even fatally ill, is high. If you have a known source for fresh, healthy meat, and the meat is handled safely, raw foods can be beneficial, but you must take precautions. You may wish to discuss this issue with your veterinarian.

supplements are a necessary part of the puppies' diet. What is actually more important is that the calcium and phosphorus are in balance. Therefore, if the puppy is eating a recipe high in meats and meat proteins (which are high in phosphorus), then a bonemeal supplement (which is high in calcium) is in order.

Feeding Pregnant Bitches

The female dogs who have the easiest time during pregnancy and nursing are those who are healthy to begin with. Prior to breeding your female dog, take her in to your veterinarian and have a thorough physical done, complete with blood work, and make sure she is in excellent health. At the same time, the vet can check her for any potential inherited problems, such as elbow or hip dysplasia, eye defects, heart problems, thyroid problems, and anything else that's common in her breed.

Then make sure she is eating an excellent diet, whether home cooked, raw, or commercial. As her pregnancy progresses (after about the sixth week of gestation), she will need more food but will have less room for it (as the growing puppies take up more space), so she will need smaller meals more often. Toward the latter part of her pregnancy, she will need to be eating 1.25 to 1.5 times her normal diet.

Feeding Nursing Moms

When she gives birth to her puppies, your mother dog may want to eat one or all of the placentas. You can talk to your veterinarian ahead of time so you know how many she should be allowed to eat. Many breeders allow the bitch to eat one or two, as the placentas do contain nutrients and hormones. However, they do not allow the bitch to eat all of them (should it be a large litter), as she could potentially make herself sick by overdoing it.

After giving birth, offer the new mom a small meal (a quarter of a cup to one cup, depending on her breed and size) of yogurt (or kefir) with a bit of honey in it. If you have access to it, you could also offer her some goat's milk with honey. (Do not give her any cow's milk, as dogs cannot digest this well.)

As her milk comes in and the puppies are nursing well, her calorie needs will increase. Initially, she will need 1.25 times her normal food in both amount and calories. However, if she has a large, rapidly growing litter, by the time the puppies are three weeks old, she could be needing 3 to 4 times her normal food in quantity and calories. To obtain this, she may need to have four or even five meals per day.

Feeding Kittens

Kittens are busy, active little creatures. They play hard and need to eat a good, nutritious diet to supply them with the energy for activity and growth.

The calorie recommendations for growing kittens are as follows:

- A one-pound kitten needs 141 calories per day.
- A two-pound kitten needs 231 calories per day.
- A three-pound kitten needs 281 calories per day.
- A four-pound kitten needs 302 calories per day.
- A five-pound kitten needs 307 calories per day.
- A six-pound kitten needs 310 calories per day.

As a general rule, a weaned, rapidly growing kitten will probably need twice as many calories at this stage of life than he will need when he's full grown and at his adult weight. When the kitten has reached 50 percent of his adult weight, he will need about 1.5 times the calories he will need as an adult. When he's at 75 percent of his adult weight, he will need only about 1.25 times his adult calorie needs.

These are only guidelines, however, as each kitten is an individual. You may find these guidelines suit your kitten wonderfully, or you may discover that your kitten is always hungry and is not gaining weight normally. If that happens, increase the calories, proteins, and fats.

Commercial Foods

As we discussed in chapter 3, commercial foods vary in quality, and that includes kitten foods. Some require the kitten to eat

Cats Are Not Born Finicky

While researching this book, I talked to cat owners and breeders about cat nutrition and recipes, and several breeders asked me to remind kitten owners that cats are not born finicky. Although cats have the reputation of being incredibly picky eaters, they become that way because they haven't been exposed to a variety of foods as kittens.

Charlene Oakley, who breeds Russian blues, said, "All of our kittens are offered a variety of different foods from weaning on until they go to new homes. They get grated carrots and squash, hard-boiled eggs, meats and fish of all kinds, and even fish eggs." She says by doing this, the kittens are assured of a balanced diet, and when they go to new homes, they will be willing to eat a variety of foods.

more food that the kitten could easily do to obtain the needed nutrition. Other kitten foods contain large amounts of cereal grains that no cat should eat. Luckily, however, today there are better foods that can nourish the kitten with quality ingredients.

A commercial food for kittens can be labeled either as a kitten food or it can be labeled for all life stages. Kitten foods tend to be higher in calories, protein, and fat. Just read the labels using the guidelines and tools set out in chapter 3 to choose a food that has nutrition your kitten needs.

Supplements

Supplements can help make sure the kitten is eating a balanced diet with no nutritional gaps. The supplements should not be counted on to create the nutritional diet, but instead, should be looked upon as a safeguard.

Supplements recommended for kittens include the following:

- a good-quality natural vitamin and mineral supplement
- a taurine supplement
- a fatty acid supplement, such as chicken fat, cod liver oil, salmon oil, fish oil, or safflower oil
- a bonemeal supplement: either natural bonemeal, finely ground eggshells, or a calcium lactate supplement
- a nutritional yeast supplement.
- a green-food supplement, such as blue-green algae, spirulina, or barley grass
- a health food blend, such as Tri-Natural Product's Missing Link for Cats

Dosages will vary according to the product and manufacturer, so read the directions carefully. The supplements should be fed with food so as not to upset the kitten's tummy.

Feeding Pregnant and Nursing Queens

Pregnant and nursing queens (mother cats are called queens) need good nutritious foods to nourish their young. They need lots of protein and fat and few carbohydrates.

The calorie recommendations for pregnant cats are as follows:

- A six-pound cat needs 273 calories per day.
- A seven-pound cat needs 318 calories per day.
- An eight-pound cat needs 364 calories per day.
- A nine-pound cat needs 409 calories per day.

- A ten-pound cat needs 455 calories per day.
- An eleven-pound cat needs 500 calories per day.

A lactating queen (nursing mom) needs a lot of calories:

- A six-pound cat needs 682 calories per day.
- A seven-pound cat needs 795 calories per day.
- An eight-pound cat needs 909 calories per day.
- A nine-pound cat needs 1,023 calories per day.
- A ten-pound cat needs 1,136 calories per day.
- An eleven-pound cat needs 1,250 calories per day.

Most cats can continue on their normal diet throughout their pregnancy and lactation. If their diet is good, they will just need some extra food in additional meals throughout the day. In addition, some high-protein treats can add some extra nutrition.

Recipes for Puppies

A Blue Dog Special . . . .

Blue Dog is an Australian cattle dog, and she thinks this recipe is awesome. And since Blue Dog can be picky, we'll take her word for it that it satisfies the canine palate.

Fast-growing, active puppies need more calories, fat, and protein than adult dogs. This recipe has about 1,500 calories.

2 cups chicken, boneless
1 cup sweet potato, chopped
4 large chicken eggs, hard-boiled, shelled

$^1/_2$ cup oatmeal, old-fashioned
$^1/_4$ cup blueberries, fresh or frozen
1 tablespoon sesame oil
1 cup raw dark greens, finely chopped (spinach, romaine
    lettuce, broccoli florets, collard greens, or a mixture
    of several)

....

1. Cut the chicken into strips for easier cooking, and cook
   until done and tender. Chop into puppy-sized bites.
2. While the meat is cooking, microwave (or boil or bake)
   the chopped sweet potato until soft and put the oatmeal on
   to cook.
3. Place the raw, finely chopped greens on a paper or
   microwave-safe plate, and cover with a wet paper towel.
   Microwave (or steam) for fifteen seconds.
4. Crumble the hard-boiled, shelled eggs into a bowl. Add
   the blueberries, oil, and cooked greens. When the meat is
   done and cut up, add it to the bowl. Add the sweet potato
   and the oatmeal when both are cooked.
5. Mix all the ingredients gently, making sure all is well
   mixed but not turned into a mush.

Divide into two, three, or four servings, depending upon how
often your puppy eats and how big (or small) he or she is. Refrigerate the remaining meals.

Suggested daily supplements include the following:

- a good-quality natural vitamin and mineral supplement
- a bonemeal supplement: either natural bonemeal, finely
  ground eggshells, or a calcium lactate supplement
- a green-food supplement, such as blue-green algae, spirulina, or barley grass

- a nutritional yeast supplement
- a health food blend, such as Springtime, Inc.'s Longevity or Tri-Natural Product's Missing Link

Supplements should be added as the food is served.

Variations (using the same amounts as for the original ingredients):

- Use safflower oil instead of sesame oil.
- Frozen dark greens can be used in place of fresh, just make sure they are thawed and cooked slightly.
- Use turkey instead of chicken.
- Use a yam instead of a sweet potato.
- Use wild brown rice instead of oatmeal.

This food will be good in the refrigerator for two to three days.

Beef and Barley...........................

This protein-rich recipe is great for puppies; the strong beef taste appeals even to fussy eaters. This recipe supplies about 1,500 calories.

2 cups beef, ground, about 90 percent lean
$^1/_2$ cup beef liver
$^1/_2$ cup barley
3 chicken eggs, hard-boiled, shelled, crumbled
1 tablespoon molasses, dark
1 tablespoon safflower oil
$^1/_3$ cup yogurt, plain

1. Place the ground beef in a skillet. Cut up the beef liver into puppy-sized bites and place in the skillet. Cook until meats are done.

2. While the meat is cooking, put the barley on to cook according to directions.
3. Place the cooked meats into a bowl. Add the cooked barley, crumbled eggs, molasses, and safflower oil. Mix thoroughly but gently.

Divide into two, three, or four servings, depending upon how
often your puppy is used to eating and the size of your puppy.
When serving, add the yogurt.

Suggested daily supplements include the following:

- a good-quality natural vitamin and mineral supplement
- a bonemeal supplement: either natural bonemeal, finely
ground eggshells, or a calcium lactate supplement
- a green-food supplement, such as blue-green algae, spirulina, or barley grass
- a nutritional yeast supplement
- a health food blend, such as Springtime, Inc.'s Longevity or
Tri-Natural Product's Missing Link

Supplements should be added as the food is served.

Variations (using the same amounts as for the original
ingredients):

- For puppies with a more sensitive digestive system, you can
substitute rice for the barley, but use wild rice or brown
rice, not white.
- To boost the nutrition and to slightly change the taste, use
two goose eggs instead of three chicken eggs.

This food will remain good in the refrigerator for two to three
days.

Recipes for Pregnant Dogs

Mother's Choice with Commercial Dog Food . . . .

As has already been discussed, not all commercial dog foods are bad; there are some excellent-quality foods available. So if you're feeding one of those foods and just want to boost your dog's nutrition with some supplemental feeding during her pregnancy, here is a recipe that can be added to most good-quality commercial dog foods without upsetting the nutritional balance. Use the variations on alternate days to provide a variety of nutrients. Depending upon the variation used, it adds between 500 and 600 calories to the dog's diet.

$^1/_2$ cup pasta
$^1/_4$ cup carrots, raw, grated
$^1/_2$ cup chicken hearts
$^1/_2$ cup chicken, deboned
1 tablespoon molasses
$^1/_2$ cup cottage cheese

---

1. Put the pasta and carrots in a saucepan, cover with water, and bring to a boil.
2. Cut the chicken hearts and chicken into bite-sized pieces and add to the water.
3. When the mixture has come to boil, turn the heat down, and cook over a medium to low heat. If the water gets low, add just enough to cover the foods in the pan. Remove from stove when the meats are thoroughly cooked.
4. Add molasses, mixing thoroughly but gently.

Divide the food (including the water it was cooked in) into as many meals as your dog is eating. Add a portion to her regular dog food, along with a portion of the cottage cheese, and mix well so that she eats it all. Refrigerate the remaining food.

Suggested daily supplements include the following:

- a good-quality natural vitamin and mineral supplement
- a fatty acid supplement, such as chicken fat, cod liver oil, salmon oil, fish oil, or safflower oil
- a bonemeal supplement: either natural bonemeal, finely ground eggshells, or a calcium lactate supplement
- a green-food supplement, such as blue-green algae, spirulina, or barley grass
- a nutritional yeast supplement
- a health food blend, such as Springtime, Inc.'s Longevity or Tri-Natural Product's Missing Link

Supplements should be added as the food is served.

Variations (using the same amounts as for the original ingredients):

- Use beef instead of the chicken and chicken hearts.
- Use beef heart instead of the chicken and chicken heart.
- Use oatmeal instead of the pasta.
- Use wild or brown rice instead of the pasta.
- Use yogurt instead of the cottage cheese.
- Use kefir instead of the cottage cheese.

Glop for Moms and Moms to Be . . . .

Dog, cat, and other small-animal breeders have been using glop for many years, so many that the origins of the name have disappeared. I suppose it's due to the sound the food makes when it drops into the bowl, glop! But in any case, glop is an excellent food to tempt the appetite.

The goat's milk in the recipe is easily tolerated even by those dogs who cannot easily digest cow's milk.

This is not a recipe for a daily food; instead this is a nutritious supplemental food that will tempt the pregnant bitch's appetite, especially if she doesn't feel good or is close to giving birth. It is also a great food to add to the daily ration of a nursing bitch.

> 2 cups water
> 2 envelopes unflavored gelatin
> 1 cup goat's milk, fresh or canned
> 1 teaspoon chicken bouillon, no- or low-salt,
>   gluten- and MSG-free
> 1 cup chicken, cooked, finely shredded

1. Place the water in a microwave-safe bowl and add the two envelopes of gelatin. Stir slightly to mix.
2. Microwave for one to two minutes or until the water is bubbling.
3. Add the remaining ingredients and stir well.
4. Refrigerate for a couple of hours until the gelatin sets.

Serve by spoonful by hand to a pregnant mom who doesn't feel good or to a new nursing mom, or just add a heaping spoonful to the mom's meals for some extra nutrition.

Variation (using the same amounts as for the original ingredients):

- Although chicken is soothing to most dogs who aren't feeling their best, many dogs are more tempted to eat beef. Substitute beef bouillon for the chicken bouillon, and one cup cooked ground beef for the chicken.

This will remain good for up to a week in the refrigerator.

Chelsea's Favorite . . . .

Chelsea, an English springer spaniel, enjoyed this diet and ate it with enthusiasm while nursing her four healthy puppies.

A nursing mother dog needs not only a lot of food, but also a good balance of proteins, carbohydrates, and fats. This daily diet (about 2,000 calories depending on the variation used), alternated with the variations listed below, will provide a fifty-pound nursing mother with excellent nutrition to provide milk for her puppies. (Always watch the puppies, though, as mother dogs can lose milk for a variety of reasons.)

2 cups pasta
1 cup oatmeal, old-fashioned, not instant
$1/2$ cup rice, wild
$1/2$ cup carrots, raw, grated
2 cups beef, muscle meat (rump roast)—no ground beef
2 cups chicken, deboned
$1/2$ cup chicken hearts
2 tablespoons molasses, dark
2 eggs, chicken, hard-boiled, shelled
$1/2$ cup cottage cheese
$1/2$ cup applesauce, unsweetened

1. Place the pasta, oatmeal, rice, and carrots in a large saucepan, cover with water, and cook until the water begins to boil.
2. Cut all of the meat into small bite-sized pieces, and add to the boiling water and previous ingredients. Cook until water comes back to a boil then lower heat and continue cooking until meat is completely cooked.
3. If the water cooks away, add some more, but only enough to cover the foods.

4. When the meat is done, take the pan off the stove. Add the molasses and crumbled eggs and mix gently.

Divide the mixture, including the water it was cooked in, into three, four, or five meals—as many as your nursing mother dog needs. Refrigerate remaining meals until mealtime. Add a portion of the cottage cheese and applesauce to each meal when serving.

Suggested daily supplements include the following:

- a good-quality natural vitamin and mineral supplement
- a fatty acid supplement, such as chicken fat, cod liver oil, salmon oil, fish oil, or safflower oil
- a bonemeal supplement: either natural bonemeal, finely ground eggshells, or a calcium lactate supplement
- a green-food supplement, such as blue-green algae, spirulina, or barley grass
- a nutritional yeast supplement
- a health food blend, such as Springtime, Inc.'s Longevity or Tri-Natural Product's Missing Link

Supplements should be added as the food is served.

Variations (using the same amounts as for the original ingredients):

- Substitute turkey for the chicken and turkey giblets for the chicken hearts.
- Substitute salmon for the chicken hearts.
- Substitute sweet potatoes for the oatmeal.
- Substitute yogurt for the cottage cheese.
- Use kefir instead of the cottage cheese.

This will remain good in the refrigerator for two to three days.

Recipes for Kittens

Squash's Special Glop. . . . .

Squash and her sister, Pumpkin, were rescued from alongside a rural road just before Halloween a few years ago. They were very small, probably no more than five weeks of age, and had been hungry for a little while. Pumpkin, the larger sister, was also a little stronger. Squash, however, needed some help right away, so with our veterinarian's okay, we made up this recipe for her, and I'm sure it helped save her life.

For an ill, injured, or recuperating kitten, this can be fed as food for a few days (with your veterinarian's okay, of course), at least long enough to get the kitten eating again. When the kitten is eating, this can be used as a supplemental food.

1 cup unflavored Pedialyte (from the infant section of
    the grocery store or drugstore)
1 three-ounce can of albacore tuna, in oil, drained
2 envelopes unflavored gelatin
1 cup goat's milk, fresh or canned
$1/2$ cup yogurt, plain, with live, active cultures
1 teaspoon molasses, dark

1. Place the Pedialyte in a bowl and add the dry gelatin. Stir to mix.
2. Cook in the microwave until the mixture is bubbling.
3. Shred the tuna well, into very small pieces, and add to the mixture. Let it cool for about fifteen mintues.
4. When it's cool but before the gelatin sets, add the remaining ingredients and mix well. (If you add the yogurt to the mixture before it cools, the heat will kill the beneficial bacteria in the yogurt.)

5. Put the bowl in the refrigerator and let set, usually a couple of hours.

Feed a small, ailing kitten a bit from your finger as often as he or she will take some. A larger kitten who is already eating can take a tablespoonful with each meal.

This food will remain good in the refrigerator for up to a week.

Variations (using the same amounts as for the original ingredients):

- Use salmon and its oil instead of the tuna.
- Use chicken and chicken fat instead of the tuna.
- Use kefir instead of the yogurt.

Taste-Tempting Turkey and Salmon. . . . .

This nutritious recipe, at about 400 calories, makes enough food for one day for a growing kitten or a very active young cat. The food can be divided into as many meals as the kitten normally eats.

$\frac{1}{2}$ cup turkey, cooked
1 three and a quarter ounce can salmon, in oil
$\frac{1}{4}$ cup rice, wild, cooked well
1 egg, chicken, large, hard-boiled and shelled
$\frac{1}{4}$ cup wheatgrass, finely chopped

1. Put the cooked turkey in a bowl and with a fork, shred the meat until it is in small pieces.
2. Add the salmon, including the oil it was packed in, and mix with the turkey.
3. Add the rice and the egg, crumbling the hard-boiled egg as you add it.

4. Put the wheatgrass on a paper plate, cover with a wet paper towel, and cook for ten seconds. Add the wheatgrass to the mixture.
5. Mix all the ingredients thoroughly.

Divide into as many servings as your kitten is used to each day. Refrigerate the remaining food until mealtimes.

Suggested daily supplements include the following:

- a good-quality natural vitamin and mineral supplement
- a taurine supplement
- a bonemeal supplement: either natural bonemeal, finely ground eggshells, or a calcium lactate supplement
- a nutritional yeast supplement
- a green-food supplement, such as blue-green algae, spirulina, or barley grass
- a health food blend, such as Tri-Natural Product's Missing Link for Cats

Supplements should be added as the food is served.

Variations (using the same amounts as for the original ingredients):

- Substitute cooked grated summer squash in place of the wild rice.
- Use grated carrots in place of the wheatgrass.
- Use chicken instead of the turkey.
- Use scrambled egg with a bit of cheddar cheese instead of the hard-boiled egg.

This recipe will remain good in the refrigerator for two to three days.

Xena's Raw Beef Special . . . .

Xena, a brown, black, and gray tabby, really enjoys this recipe. This recipe supplies about 350 calories. As was mentioned earlier in this chapter, feed raw meats to queens and kittens only when you have a reliable source of clean, healthy meats.

1 cup beef, raw, muscle meat, finely chopped
$^1/_4$ cup tuna, raw, finely chopped
1 egg, chicken, raw
1 tablespoon wheatgrass, finely chopped
1 tablespoon yogurt, plain, regular

1. Mix the first three ingredients, stirring well.
2. Put the wheatgrass on a paper plate and cover with a wet paper towel. Microwave for five seconds to lightly steam the grass. Add to the meat mixture and stir.

Divide into as many meals as your kitten usually eats; refrigerate the remaining meals until serving. Add a portion of the yogurt when serving.

Suggested supplements include the following:

- a good-quality natural vitamin and mineral supplement
- a taurine supplement
- a fatty acid supplement, such as chicken fat, cod liver oil, salmon oil, fish oil, or safflower oil
- a bonemeal supplement: either natural bonemeal, finely ground eggshells, or a calcium lactate supplement
- a nutritional yeast supplement
- a green-food supplement, such as blue-green algae, spirulina, or barley grass

- a health food blend, such as Tri-Natural Product's Missing Link for Cats

Add the supplements when serving the food.

Variations (using the same amounts as for the original ingredients):

- Use another type of fish instead of the tuna.
- Use clams or oysters instead of the tuna.
- Use fresh spinach instead of the wheatgrass.
- Use kefir instead of the yogurt.

Recipes for Pregnant and Nursing Momma Cats

Momma Cat's Nutritious Glop . . . .

Pregnant and nursing momma cats often don't feel like eating. Unfortunately, if they stop eating, their health can suffer as well as that of their kittens. Glop can be a potential lifesaver, as we've shown in other situations. This high-protein glop is great for pregnant and nursing queens. Use this recipe to get extra nutrition into a cat but do not use it as a daily diet.

    1 cup unflavored Pedialyte (from the infant section
        of the grocery store or drugstore)
    1 three-ounce can of albacore tuna, in oil, drained
    2 eggs, chicken, hard-boiled, finely crumbled
    2 envelopes unflavored gelatin
    1 cup goat's milk, fresh or canned
    1/2 cup yogurt, plain, with live, active cultures
    1 teaspoon molasses, dark

1. Place the Pedialyte in a bowl and add the dry gelatin. Stir to mix.
2. Cook in the microwave until the mixture is bubbling.
3. Shred the tuna well, into very small pieces, crumble the hard-boiled eggs, and add both to the mixture. Let it cool for about fifteen minutes.
4. When it's cool but before the gelatin sets, add the remaining ingredients and mix well. (If you add the yogurt to the mixture before it cools, the heat will kill the beneficial bacteria in the yogurt.)
5. Put the bowl in the refrigerator and let set, usually a couple of hours.

Feed both pregnant and nursing cats a tablespoon as often as they will take it when they are showing no signs of an appetite. If they are eating, but not much, use a tablespoon of this several times a day as a supplement to their regular food.

This food will remain good in the refrigerator for up to a week.

Variations (using the same amounts as for the original ingredients):

- Use salmon and its oil instead of the tuna.
- Use chicken and chicken fat instead of the tuna.
- Use kefir instead of the yogurt.

A Protein Treat . . . .

Nursing moms need good nutrition to produce enough milk for their babies, and mother cats are no exception. Far too many momma cats are just skin and bones by the time their kittens are weaned. Although it's good that their babies are fat and healthy, this depleted condition leaves the momma cats susceptible to illness when they have given so much to their kittens.

This high-protein, meat-based treat is crunchy, tasty, and has been accepted by almost all of the cats who did taste tests for me. As a treat (and not a regular food) it just adds a bit of additional nutrition to the mother cat's daily diet.

1 pound finely chopped chicken livers and hearts
2 eggs, chicken, large
$^1/_2$ cup flour, barley, finely ground
$^1/_4$ cup flaxseed meal, finely ground
$^1/_2$ chicken broth with fat

1. Put the chicken livers and hearts in a food processor, and liquefy until a thick paste. If you need to, do it in two batches, and add just enough chicken broth so that it can process.
2. Put the processed chicken into a bowl and add the eggs, flour, and flaxseed meal. Stir until well mixed. The dough should be stiff, but if it's too difficult to work, add a bit of chicken broth.
3. Place the dough on a cookie sheet in pea-sized (bite-sized) balls.
4. Make a tiny indentation in the top of each treat and place a drop or two of the remaining chicken broth in each indentation.
5. Bake at 350 degrees for six to eight minutes or until the bottoms of the treats are golden brown.

Remove from the oven, let cool, and then store in an airtight container in the refrigerator. A few of these treats can be added to each meal, and a few offered here and there throughout the day.

These treats will stay good in the refrigerator for a couple of weeks.

CHAPTER NINE

Recipes for
Active, Performance,
and Working Dogs

Each individual dog has his or her own nutritional needs. These can be based on the animal's age, activity level, and state of health, as well as on the sport the dog participates in or his or her occupation. This chapter has several recipes (home cooked and raw) for adult dogs, including active pets, as well as very active, hardworking ones.

I suggest that you try many of the recipes in this book and keep notes in your journal or on your calendar as to how well your dog liked the recipe, what gastrointestinal results occurred (if any), and whether you would like to make it again. Then when you find three, four, or five recipes you and your pet both like, make those regularly. By varying the recipes and ingredients, you prevent your pet from getting bored, and the variety of the ingredients will add to your pet's good nutritional health.

The Active Dog

The average dog goes for a walk every day, plays a couple of times each day, and then is relatively calm the rest of the day; the active dog is busier than that. The active dog patrols the backyard looking for birds, squirrels, or trespassers. He or she will also go check out the front door or window when someone walks by. He or she may go for a jog with Dad each morning and later in the day go for a jog while Mom rides her bicycle.

The active dog might also be in training, either for conformation or obedience competition, or for agility or herding. He may be under some stress, too, because of the training and may need some extra calories to cope with that.

The active dog is going to need a few more calories each day as well as some increased protein. How many calories is going to vary significantly depending upon the dog's activities. If you find your dog is losing weight and doesn't have enough energy for training, work, or play, then increase his calories. If he's gaining weight, then he's getting too many and the calories need to be decreased.

Here are some general guidelines for the calorie needs of active dogs:

- A 10-pound dog needs 450 to 600 calories per day.
- A 20-pound dog needs 750 to 900 calories per day.
- A 35-pound dog needs 1,200 to 1,400 calories per day.
- A 50-pound dog needs 1,400 to 1,650 calories per day.
- A 70-pound dog needs 1,800 to 2,100 calories per day.
- A 90-pound dog needs 2,200 to 2,500 calories per day.

- A 100-pound dog needs 2,500 to 2,700 calories per day.
- A 120-pound dog needs 2,900 to 3,300 calories per day.
- A 150-pound dog needs 3,500 to 4,000 calories per day.

Commercial Foods

Many active dogs can thrive on a commercial food, as long as it's an excellent-quality food. Check the calorie measurements on the label of the food to see if the amount of food your dog is eating should be increased to meet his calorie needs.

However, if your dog seems to run out of steam midway through a play session or is not able to continue jogging with you like he or she used to, you can check with the veterinarian to make sure there is no other problem (such as a thyroid problem or hip dyplasia), and you can increase the amount of food he's eating.

Supplements

The supplement needs of an active dog don't necessarily need to change as long as the dog's diet is very good. However, as with all dogs, the supplements should be fed to assure there are no nutritional gaps in the diet.

If you have been feeding your dog a supplement program that is working well, but you have increased his activities through exercise, training, or play, continue with those same supplements and simply increase his diet.

The Outside Dog

Dogs who live outside for most or all of the year, or who spend a great deal of time outside, may need additional nutritional support. During the cold months when the temperature drops, the dog will need additional calories so that he can maintain his body temperature.

Although individual dogs will have different abilities to cope depending upon breed, coat type and thickness, age, and state of health, as a general rule the dog's nutrition should be increased as the temperature drops.

- At fifty degrees Fahrenheit, feed normally.
- At forty degrees Fahrenheit, increase calories by 10 to 15 percent (from normal).
- At thirty degrees Fahreheit, increase calories by 15 to 25 percent (from normal).
- At twenty degrees Fahrenheit, increase calories by 30 to 40 percent (from normal).
- At ten degrees Fahrenheit, increase calories by 45 to 55 percent (from normal).
- At zero degrees Fahrenheit, increase calories by 65 to 75 percent (from normal).

In northern states where the temperature may be very low for days on end, dogs who spend all their time outside may even need to have their calorie intake doubled. If you have any questions about your dog's nutritional needs in regard to cold weather, talk to your veterinarian.

Those dogs who live in warmer climates face a different challenge. Many dogs do not like to eat when it's hot and may vegetate all day during the worst of the heat, only to wake up and resume activities when the sun goes down and the air cools. These dogs will need fewer calories, although how many fewer will depend upon the individual dog, how much the

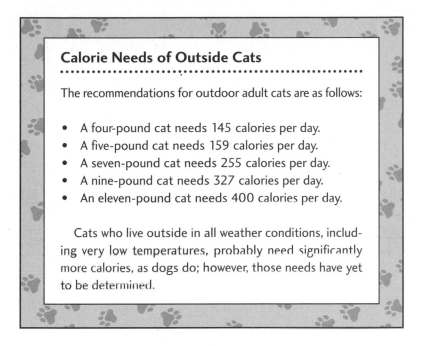

Calorie Needs of Outside Cats

The recommendations for outdoor adult cats are as follows:

- A four-pound cat needs 145 calories per day.
- A five-pound cat needs 159 calories per day.
- A seven-pound cat needs 255 calories per day.
- A nine-pound cat needs 327 calories per day.
- An eleven-pound cat needs 400 calories per day.

Cats who live outside in all weather conditions, including very low temperatures, probably need significantly more calories, as dogs do; however, those needs have yet to be determined.

dog's sleeping, and how active he or she is when the air cools. These dogs will also appreciate being fed at night. Don't forget the water, though; dogs who must tolerate hot weather need lots of cool water available all the time.

The Performance or Working Dog

Dogs who compete in very active sports, such as sled-dog racing, and dogs who work hard for a living, like search-and-rescue dogs or ranch dogs, need significantly more calories when they're working hard. The calories can come from protein, fats, and some carbohydrates, but the calories from fats are most easily metabolized. In addition, working-dog performance is significantly better on a high-fat diet versus a high-carbohydrate one; the blood sugar is more stable—without peaks and valleys—and the dog doesn't get as tired so quickly. Susan Donoghue, VMD, says, "Dietary fats are high octane fuel, providing, ounce for ounce, 2.5 times the calories of protein and carbohydrates."

The problem is that these dogs don't work hard each and every day, consistently, and if fed a diet high in protein, fats, and carbohydrates all the time, even these dogs will gain weight. A balance must be reached so that high-performance dogs can eat a good-quality diet every day and then have some supplemental nutrition before, during, and after high-performance work.

"The biggest key to good nutrition during performance is to begin feeding your dog prior to competition season," says Jocelynn Jacobs, DVM, of Freeland, Michigan, who breeds, shows, and races her AKC Alaskan malamutes, and who is also the author of *Performance Dog Nutrition* (Sno Shire Publications, 2005). Jacobs emphasizes that quality is just as important (or more important) than quantity. "If a poor quality food is fed during the off season, one that doesn't supply all the needed amino acids, for example, then the dog's body will be forced to take protein from existing muscles to meet its needs."

The Downside to Fats

Increase the fat content of your dog's food very slowly prior to the time when your dog will need that extra energy. Too much fat added to the diet too quickly—the night before a competition, for example—will cause diarrhea. Often very potent diarrhea!

Unused fats will be stored in your dog's body. So if your dog is getting too much in his or her diet that isn't being used, your dog may begin to gain weight. You're going to have to constantly watch your dog and evaluate his dietary needs.

You can add fats to your dog's diet by doing one or more of the following:

- Use meats and meat cuts with more fat on them.
- Use ground beef or bison with higher fat contents.
- Use duck or goose instead of chicken.
- Add slightly more oil to your dog's diet; the key is "slightly," as too much oil will cause diarrhea.
- Add goat's cheese or yogurt to the diet.

Calorie Needs

The calorie needs of a performance or working dog will probably remain within the guidelines established for an active dog except when under stress, when training hard for performance, or during actual work or performance situations.

If your dog is tired, doesn't have enough energy to train or perform, or gives up in situations where he normally would not, then his diet may be letting him down and it should be reevaluated.

Some general guidelines for hardworking and performance dogs are as follows:

- A 20-pound dog needs 750 to 1,000 calories per day.
- A 35-pound dog needs 1,400 to 1,650 calories per day.
- A 50-pound dog needs 1,600 to 2,000 calories per day.
- A 70-pound dog needs 1,900 to 2,300 calories per day.
- A 90-pound dog needs 2,500 to 3,000 calories per day.
- A 100-pound dog needs 2,600 to 3,200 calories per day.
- A 120-pound dog needs 3,000 to 3,700 calories per day.
- A 150-pound dog needs 3,500 to 4,300 calories per day.

Commercial Foods

Very few commercial foods are able to supply the numbers of calories hardworking dogs need. A dog would have to be able to eat many more cups of food than normal, and he physically wouldn't be able to do it.

The owners of many hardworking dogs, including racing sled dogs, for example, use a good-quality commercial food as a foundation and then supplement that food with meat and fat to add the extra calories. It takes considerable practice to figure out exactly how much extra food any particular dog will need. To figure out each dog's needs, the owner will watch the dog's activity levels, ability to run for extended periods of time, the dog's ability to recuperate after exertion, and the dog's body weight.

An Excellent Commercial Dog Food

Evo, made by Natura Pet products, is advertised as, "The ancestral diet meets modern nutrition." This is a grain-free, low-carbohydrate, high-protein diet that has the potential to meet the needs of many active, performance, and working dogs. Ingredients include turkey, chicken, turkey meal, chicken meal, potatoes, herring meal, chicken fat, egg, apples, tomatoes, carrots, garlic, cottage cheese, and more. Protein is no less than 42 percent; fat is no less than 22 percent; fiber is no more than 2.5 percent; moisture is no more than 10 percent; and carbohydrates are no more than 12 percent. The Web site is www.naturapet.com.

Recipes for the Active Dog

Beef and Rice ....

This recipe supplies 1,500 calories and a nice balance of protein, fat, and carbohydrates for an active fifty-pound dog.

....

    1 cup beef, ground or cubed
    6 ounces beef heart, cubed
    $^1/_2$ cup rice, wild
    $^1/_2$ cup oatmeal, old-fashioned, not instant
    2 tablespoons safflower oil
    4 eggs, chicken, large, hard-boiled, shelled

....

1. Sauté the cubed beef and beef hearts over a low to medium fire until well done. If needed, add a little oil to the pan to prevent scorching.
2. While the meat is cooking, cook the rice and oatmeal (separately or in the same pan).
3. When the beef, rice, and oatmeal are all done, place all in a bowl. Scrape the pan the beef was cooked in, putting all the leftover grease and meat juices into the mixture.
4. Add the safflower oil and mix well.

Divide into two servings and crumble two hard-boiled eggs over the top of each serving. Store the food in the refrigerator.

Suggested daily supplements (see chapter 6) include the following:

- a good-quality natural vitamin and mineral supplement

- a bonemeal supplement: either natural bonemeal, finely ground eggshells, or a calcium lactate supplement
- a green-food supplement, such as blue-green algae, spirulina, or barley grass
- a nutritional yeast supplement
- a health food blend, such as Springtime, Inc.'s Longevity or Tri-Natural Product's Missing Link

Supplements should be added as the food is served.
Food will remain good for two to three days in the refrigerator.
Variations (using the same amounts as for the original ingredients):

- For a slightly different taste, hard-boil two goose eggs instead of four chicken eggs, and crumble one egg over each serving.
- Use bison and bison heart instead of beef.

Beef, Bison, and Beans in the Slow Cooker . . . .

This recipe supplies about 1,500 calories and a nice balance of protein, carbohydrates, and fat for an active dog. If you find your dog doesn't metabolize beans well, try one of the other variations listed below.

3 cups beef, ground, crumbled
1 cup bison, ground, crumbled
$^1/_2$ cup red kidney beans, canned, low sodium
$^1/_4$ cup tomatoes, diced finely
$^1/_2$ cup goat cheese, crumbled

1. Brown the beef and bison until the meat is thoroughly cooked. (You can cook the meats together in the same pan.)

2. Place the beef and bison mixture in the slow cooker, add the beans and tomatoes, and cover with enough water to just cover them.
3. With the cooker on low, the ingredients can simmer all day.

Divide the cooked foods in half, keeping the water and juices, too, and store in the refrigerator. When serving, sprinkle the goat cheese on top.

Suggested daily supplements (see chapter 6) include the following:

- a good-quality natural vitamin and mineral supplement
- a fatty acid supplement, such as chicken fat, cod liver oil, salmon oil, fish oil, or safflower oil
- a bonemeal supplement: either natural bonemeal, finely ground eggshells, or a calcium lactate supplement
- a green-food supplement, such as blue-green algae, spirulina, or barley grass
- a nutritional yeast supplement
- a health food blend, such as Springtime, Inc.'s Longevity or Tri-Natural Product's Missing Link

Supplements should be added as the food is served.

Food will remain good in the refrigerator for two to three days.

Variations (using the same amounts as for the original ingredients):

- Use canned or fresh green beans, chopped, instead of the red kidney beans.
- Use grated summer squash instead of the kidney beans.
- Use grated zucchini instead of the kidney beans.

Recipes for the Performance Dog

Friday Night Fish Special . . . .

Hardworking dogs and competitive performance dogs need a special diet. These dogs burn up energy at an amazing rate while working, training, and competing, and their daily food must replenish that. Because this recipe is high in carbohydrates and fats, however, the amount fed each day must reflect that day's activity level. If the dog is going to be (or has been) working hard, increase the amounts fed. If the dog is going to have a few days off to relax and recuperate, decrease the amount of food fed.

This recipe, at about 2,100 calories, is for a very hardworking fifty-pound dog: an agility competitor who is competing in a tournament, a working herding dog on a ranch, or a search-and-rescue dog who trains and works hard every day.

....

    1 pound mackerel, raw, deboned
    2 eggs, goose
    1 cup pasta
    1/4 cup spinach, fresh, finely chopped
    1/4 cup romaine lettuce, finely chopped
    1/4 cup carrots, finely grated
    2 tablespoons safflower oil
    1 tablespoon flaxseed meal, finely grated
    1/2 cup cheese, cheddar, grated

....

1. Preheat oven to 450 degrees.
2. Wrap the mackerel in foil, place in baking pan, and bake until done, usually about ten minutes per inch of thickness of the fish.

3. While the fish is cooking, put the pasta in a saucepan, and cook until soft.
4. When the fish is done, pull the pan out of the oven, unwrap the fish, and pull it apart (carefully, it's hot) until the fish is completely shredded.
5. When the pasta is done, drain off most of the water, and add the pasta to the fish in the pan.
6. Add the greens, carrots, and flaxseed meal to the fish and pasta.
7. Crack the two goose eggs over the pasta and fish, and then stir the mixture, breaking the egg yolks and making sure everything is well mixed.
8. Sprinkle the cheddar cheese over the mixture.
9. Put back in the oven and bake for about ten minutes or until the eggs are thoroughly cooked and the cheese is melted.

Remove the pan from the oven and let the food cool. Divide into two or three meals (as many as your dog is used to eating in a day). Store in the refrigerator.

Suggested daily supplements include the following:

- a good-quality natural vitamin and mineral supplement
- a bonemeal supplement: either natural bonemeal, finely ground eggshells, or a calcium lactate supplement
- a green-food supplement, such as blue-green algae, spirulina, or barley grass
- a nutritional yeast supplement
- a health food blend, such as Springtime, Inc.'s Longevity or Tri-Natural Product's Missing Link

Supplements should be added as the food is served.
Food will remain good in the refrigerator for two to three days.

Variations (using the same amounts as for the original ingredients):

- Substitute another cold-water, oil-rich fish in place of the mackerel.
- Substitute mozzarella cheese in place of the cheddar cheese.

Beef, Bacon, and Potato . . . .

This recipe supplies 1,700 calories for a fifty-pound active adult dog who is training or working hard.

> 2 cups beef, muscle meat, not ground
> 1 1/2 cups sweet potato, raw
> 1/4 cup bacon, cooked, crumbled
> 1/2 cup carrots, raw, grated
> 1 three-ounce can of salmon in oil
> 1 cup yogurt

1. Cut the beef into small bite-sized pieces, and put in a large saucepan.
2. Chop the sweet potato into small bite-sized pieces, and add to the pan.
3. Add the carrots and then enough water to just cover the ingredients. Turn the heat on high until the water begins to bubble. Turn the heat down to medium-low, and let cook until the meat is done and the sweet potatoes are soft.
4. Remove from heat. Add the salmon and bacon, and mix well.

Divide into two or three meals (as many as your dog is used to eating each day) and refrigerate. When serving, add a portion of the yogurt.

Suggested daily supplements (see chapter 6) include the following:

- a good-quality natural vitamin and mineral supplement
- a bonemeal supplement: either natural bonemeal, finely ground eggshells, or a calcium lactate supplement
- a green-food supplement, such as blue-green algae, spirulina, or barley grass
- a nutritional yeast supplement
- a health food blend, such as Springtime, Inc.'s Longevity or Tri-Natural Product's Missing Link

Supplements should be added as the food is served.

Food will stay good in the refrigerator for two to three days.

CHAPTER TEN

Recipes for
Pets with Special Needs

What your pet eats can affect his body in many ways. For example, when a dog who has a food sensitivity to wheat eats a commercial dog biscuit made primarily of wheat, he may begin licking and chewing at his paws or at the base of his tail, and he may be itchy everywhere. When you pet him, his skin may flinch under your hands because he's so itchy.

What our pets eat is also important as they age, as the nutritional requirements of senior dogs and cats change. The correct foods can also help your pet cope with some illnesses. In reality, food affects just about every part of your pet's life in some way.

Obesity: A Growing Problem

I'm not trying to be funny; obesity is a growing problem, not just for people but also for our pets, and it is increasing rapidly. Up to

45 percent of all dogs and 20 percent of all cats today are obese. Some experts feel that more pets are obese today than ever before because more pet owners are obese as well. Perhaps they are spending too much time in front of the television or the computer and are not spending enough time walking or playing with their pet. This is a debilitating and serious problem, and our dogs and cats are not born this way; the problem occurs when too many calories are taken in and too few are used.

The largest pet insurer, Veterinary Pet Insurance (VPI), paid out more than $14 million in 2006 for claims associated with pet obesity. Obesity raises the risk of joint problems, disc disease, back problems, diabetes, hypertension, hepatitis, and more.

Unfortunately, many times obesity begins because people are trying too hard to be kind to their pets. Dog treats or extra servings of dinner become signs of affection (food is love!), and the dog or cat begins to gain weight. Many pets—dogs and cats—like food and enjoy this special attention and so begin to beg for even more treats. When owners give in, a vicious cycle has begun, and the pet gains even more weight.

Although some pet owners blame their pet's weight gain on spaying or neutering their pet, that is not entirely correct. Yes, the spayed female dog or neutered male may eventually be a little less active than he or she was when younger, but that often happens even with intact (not spayed or neutered) dogs and cats. When they grow up, many pets are simply not as active as they were when they were younger. Weight gain is due to taking in too many calories and not using (through exercise) enough.

Free feeding can also be a part of this problem. If food is left out all the time and the dog or cat can nibble all day long, way too much food may be eaten. Some pets will continue to eat even when they aren't hungry; if there is food available, it will be eaten. For these pets, scheduled meals with a measured amount of food is very important.

The Ideal Body

Pets are considered obese when they weigh 15 percent or more than they should. Although pet owners can weigh their pets to determine how heavy they are, the best way to judge whether a pet is overweight is to simply look at the pet and feel him.

A dog should have a waistline. When you feel his body, he should have some meat over his bones, which should not be prominent, but you should be able to feel the ribs under the muscles. He should have a tuck up (waist) when viewed from the side.

Cats don't have waists like dogs do, or at least, not as easily seen. However, the cat, like the dog, should have meat over his bones, but you should be able to feel the ribs under the muscles.

In addition, both dogs and cats should have the energy for play. If they move around for just a few minutes and then quit, or refuse to get up to play at all, then you have a potential problem.

Before beginning a weight-loss program with your pet, talk to your veterinarian. Weight gain can be caused by some illnesses, including diabetes and hypothyroidism, and your vet may want to do some blood work to rule out these problems first.

Shawn Messonnier, DVM, says, "If your dog or cat needs to lose weight, he should be on a natural, wholesome, homemade diet." He added that the treatment of obesity requires a controlled low-calorie diet with a sensible exercise plan.

Start Walking Your Dog

The easiest way to begin an exercise program is to start walking. An obese pet may not have much muscle tone and may not be used to exercise, so walking is an easy way to get those muscles working again.

Depending on your dog's age, state of health, state of obesity, and fitness level, you may initially just walk up the block and back. That's okay; it's a start. Jot on your calendar or in your journal how far you walked and how long it took. Jot down, too, your dog's reactions. Was she happy? Did just that walk take a lot out of her? Was she out of breath? Or did she want to do more?

Initially you may want to walk your dog just once a day, especially if she's really out of shape and obese. However, if your dog can do it, and if you have the time, add a second walk so that you're walking morning and evening, or at lunchtime and in the evening, so your dog gets two good walks. She can then burn twice the calories.

Gradually increase the distance you walk and, just as slowly, increase the speed you walk. Just remember that sore muscles are no fun, not for you or for your dog. And sore muscles aren't necessary. That old adage, No pain, no gain, is not true. When the muscles are sore, that means they have been damaged, and they don't need to be hurt to gain strength.

Get the Cat Moving

It's much easier to walk a fat dog than it is to get a fat cat moving. An obese cat can be quite a bump on a log, a furball on the sofa! But your cat needs exercise, too, and you need to get him up and moving.

One way to motivate even the fattest cat is called environ-mental enrichment. Feed your cat a portion of his meals in his normal place, but divide the rest up and hide them. In the beginning, hide them in places that will be easy for him to find and help him discover them. One portion can be on the floor under the dining room table and another can be on the end table near the sofa. Later, as he gets used to moving around and searching, you can hide the food portions in more difficult places, even in the back rooms of the house. This gets your cat up and moving and, in addition, makes life more interesting.

Once your cat is again used to moving around, you may be able to get him used to playing with toys again. A feather on the end of a fishing pole makes for great fun, for you and for your cat! There are a great many other toys for cats that will help him move and burn calories; some are interactive toys that you use to play with your cat and others the cat can play with alone. Get a few of each type and then vary them to keep the games interesting and fun.

A dog who wants to go for a walk can be quite insistent; cats who need to play often are not. Make a play date with your cat so that each day at a specific time, you will play with her. In a very short period of time, you'll notice that your cat will come looking for you when it's time for your play date!

Allergies

Allergies are common problems in both people and dogs, and to a lesser extent, in cats. The allergies may be airborne and breathed in (such as pollens and dust), they may be contact (grass, mold, and mildew), or the body may react to foods that are eaten. Some pets may react to a specific ingredient in the food (such as an artificial additive or a single ingredient) and not the food as a whole.

Some pets may develop food intolerances. In these cases dogs or cats may suffer from some gastrointestinal upset when they eat a specific food. This isn't a true allergy but is often treated as such.

When an allergy or a food intolerance is suspected, it's best to consult with your veterinarian. Some medical treatments can help relieve the allergy symptoms so your pet can get some rest from the itching, chewing, and distress. Your veterinarian may also recommend allergy tests. If your budget can afford these tests, it's a great idea because you then know specifically what your pet is allergic to.

Some of the most common signs of an allergy or food intolerance include the following:

- scratching and itching with no signs of another cause (such as fleas)
- excessive licking of the paws, often causing a red stain on the fur
- chewing at the base of the tail
- poor skin (excessive dander and flaking) and a thin, dull coat
- gastrointestinal discomfort, which may include flatulence (gas), bloating, restlessness, diarrhea

Feeding Trials

If you suspect your pet has a food allergy, most veterinarians recommend feeding your dog or cat a different food with only one protein, one fat, and one carbohydrate. When you choose a protein, fat, and carbohydrate that he may not have eaten in the past, this can potentially eliminate any foods causing a reaction in his system.

There are commercial foods made specifically for pets like this. Old Mother Hubbard's Wellness line of foods has a Duck and Potato dog food with duck as the only protein source and potatoes as the only carbohydrate. They also produce a Fish and Sweet Potato dog food that has the one protein and one carbohydrate. Natural Balance Pet Foods has a Venison and Green Pea Allergy Formula for Cats.

You can also feed your dog or cat a homemade diet (cooked or raw) with limited sources of protein and carbohydrates. The Bison and Millet diet for dogs at the end of this chapter has only bison as the protein and millet as the carbohydrate. In addition, these are two foods that many dogs do not normally eat so they have the potential for being new foods that have not caused an allergy problem in the past.

The key to making these diets work is they have to be fed for at least eight weeks. During that time, there can be no other foods given to the pet. Treats must be a couple pieces of the food itself, no extras. At the end of eight weeks, you can then reevaluate your pet. Has the chewing on the feet stopped? Has the scratching stopped? If it has, then you can be pretty sure something in your pet's previous diet caused the problem.

Now, to find out what the specific ingredient is, you need to continue on the allergy diet, but once a week, add a new ingredient. So, for example, if you're feeding the Bison and Millet diet, add some beef to it for each meal during week 1. If there is no scratching, itching, or chewing, then beef isn't the problem. On Monday of week 2, stop feeding beef and add some chicken. By continuing along these lines, you should be able to isolate the foods that cause the allergic reactions. All supplements should be tested this way also, adding them back into your pet's diet one at a time, one per week.

Cereal-Grain Allergies

Many pets develop allergies to cereal grains, primarily because these are not natural foods for them. Allergies to wheat and wheat products are very common, as are allergies to corn and corn products and rice and rice products.

The pet-food recalls of 2007 also alerted us to the predominance of cereal grain glutens in foods, which are added to pet foods to boost the nutritional balance; they add plant proteins to the food. Essentially, the nutritional analysis can then show a higher protein level. Many dogs and cats, however, have difficulties processing glutens.

There are many recipes in this book with no grains and/or no glutens, and there are a few more listed at the end of this chapter.

Arthritis

Arthritis is a degenerative disease of the joints. Although thought to be limited to the joints, the immune system is very much involved, as a weakened immune system is unable to prevent the inflammation in the joints. It can be very common in dogs as they get older but is rare in cats, although we have no idea why.

Glucosamine chondroitin supplements are recommended for pets suffering from arthritis, and they have their best effect when the arthritis is in its early stages. These are cartilage protective compounds, which help the natural cartilage rebuild itself and so protect the joint from additional damage. Bovine cartilage has also been effective in relieving the pain and inflammation of arthritis, and in increasing joint mobility.

Robert Goldstein, VMD, recommends an antioxidant program for pets with arthritis, suggesting that it should include vitamins A, C, and E, as well as manganese. Joan Weiskopf, MS, a veterinary nutritionist, suggests avoiding foods in the nightshade family, which includes peppers, eggplant, potatoes, and tomatoes.

Diabetes

Diabetes is a debilitating disease. Before considering nutritional therapy for your pet, discuss the pet's disease with your veterinarian. As a general rule, dogs tend to have type I diabetes (insulin-dependent) and cats tend to have type II (non-insulin-dependent). However, there are exceptions to every rule.

Many holistic veterinarians feel that feeding cats (and potentially even dogs) a high-carbohydrate commercial food can lead to developing type II diabetes. I haven't found any studies yet to confirm this, so at this point it's still conjecture. However, cats are true carnivores and, other than for a source of fiber, do not need carbohydrates.

Dogs and cats with diabetes should eat three to four small meals per day, and the recipes should be high in fiber. This will help keep blood sugars at a more even keel rather than having huge blood sugar peaks and crashes.

Heart Disease

Heart disease is an umbrella term that refers to any of the many diseases that can affect the heart. This can range from congenital heart defects (the pet was born with it) to the aging dog's or cat's heart failure. Any pet with a heart problem should be under a veterinarian's care and guidance.

In most situations, the diet for a dog or cat with heart disease should be low in salts. Salts cause the body to retain water, which causes added strain on the heart. In addition, the excess water will leak from blood vessels and will put a strain on the other organs in the body.

Kidney Disease

Kidney disease or kidney failure usually strikes older dogs and cats, and is one of the most common causes of death in pets over ten years of age. For many years, experts have recommended that the diets of dogs and cats with kidney disease be changed from a normal diet to one of the commercial diets specifically formulated for kidney disease. However, no changes in survival rates have been documented.

The ideal diet for dogs and cats with kidney disease is one with easily digested proteins, enough vegetables to bind phosphorus in the digestive tract, and a good supply of vitamins and minerals.

Liver Disease

Liver disease is very difficult to treat; there are few medications that actually treat the causes of liver disease. However, a good diet with supplements can provide considerable support for a dog or cat with liver disease. In addition, the herbal foods milk thistle, licorice root, and red clover are excellent supplements for dogs and cats with liver disease.

Feeding Senior Dogs and Cats

In years past, it was thought that senior dogs and cats should be fed foods significantly lower in proteins. Diets that were too high in protein were thought to stress the kidneys. Unfortunately, many years of these diets and a steady increase in kidney disease have not shown this line of thought to be true.

Today, most nutrition experts, including veterinary nutritionist Joan Weiskopf, agree that senior dogs and cats need proteins that are more easily digested, but they also need high levels of proteins in their diet because the body becomes less efficient at metabolizing those proteins. A daily supplement of digestive enzymes (such as yogurt) will also help the aging body use those proteins more efficiently.

The supplement suggestions listed throughout this book are of particular benefit to the older dog and cat. A good supplement routine for older dogs should include the following:

- a good-quality natural vitamin and mineral supplement, including good, strong antioxidants
- a glucosamine and chondroitin supplement
- a fatty acid supplement, such as chicken fat, cod liver oil, salmon oil, fish oil, or safflower oil
- a bonemeal supplement: either natural bonemeal, finely ground eggshells, or a calcium lactate supplement
- a nutritional yeast supplement

- a teaspoon (for a small dog) to a tablespoon (for a large dog) of yogurt with live, active cultures
- a green-food supplement, such as blue-green algae, spirulina, or barley grass
- a health food blend, such as Springtime, Inc.'s Tonic Blend or Tri-Natural Product's Missing Link

Many of the recipes listed in this book will suit older dogs quite well, including the following:

- Bison and Millet in chapter 4
- Beef and Cheddar in chapter 4
- Turkey, Egg, and Sweet Potato in chapter 4
- Reba's Rabbit Favorite in chapter 5
- Bison and Barley in this chapter
- Antioxidant Special in this chapter
- Beef, Chicken, and Goat Cheese in this chapter
- Turkey, Barley, and Kefir in this chapter
- Chicken, Eggs, and Goat Cheese in this chapter

The supplements recommended for older cats include many of the same ones recommended for younger cats with a couple of additions. A good supplement regime for older cats should include the following:

- a good-quality natural vitamin and mineral supplement
- a taurine supplement
- a bonemeal supplement: either natural bonemeal, finely ground eggshells, or a calcium lactate supplement
- a nutritional yeast supplement
- a fish oil or cod liver oil supplement

- a teaspoon of yogurt with live active cultures
- a green-food supplement, such as blue-green algae, spirulina, or barley grass
- a health food blend, such as Tri-Natural Product's Missing Link for Cats

Many of the recipes in this chapter as well as others from throughout this book can be great for the older cat. They include the following:

- Chicken and Tuna Delight in chapter 4
- Raw-food recipe Tigger's Oyster Delight in chapter 5
- Duck and Oatmeal in this chapter
- Raw Clams for Cats in this chapter
- Chicken and Trout in this chapter

Older dogs and cats have very individual needs. Some slow down as they age, and these pets will need fewer calories so they don't gain weight. Other older pets remain amazingly active up into their older years; these pets can continue to eat as they wish as long as they don't gain too much weight. Preventing the older dog and cat from gaining weight is just as important as it is with younger pets.

It is also important to keep older dogs and cats moving. They may want to sleep in the sun, letting it warm their old bones, and a certain amount of that is fine. However, if they sleep too much, they'll lose joint mobility and muscle tone. So keep those old dogs and cats walking and playing.

Recipes for Dogs

Chicken and Apple Casserole. . . . .

This recipe makes a tasty, appealing casserole that is about 900 calories and is one day's ration for a forty- to fifty-pound adult dog who is sendentary or slightly overweight.

....

2 cups chicken, deboned
1 cup chicken broth, low sodium
1 apple, medium-sized, diced finely
$^1/_2$ cup rice, wild
$^1/_2$ cup green beans, fresh, chopped
    into small pieces
$^1/_2$ cup carrots, raw, grated
$^1/_2$ cup cheese, mozzarella, grated

....

1. Preheat oven to 350 degrees.
2. Place the diced apple in a layer on the bottom of a casserole pan.
3. Layer the wild rice next, then green beans, and carrots.
4. Cut the chicken into bite-sized pieces, and then place it in a layer over the previous ingredients. Add the chicken broth.
5. Cover with grated cheese.
6. Bake for about one hour or until the chicken is thoroughly cooked. Remove from heat and let cool.

Divide into two meals and store in the refrigerator.

Suggested daily supplements include the following:

- a good-quality natural vitamin and mineral supplement
- a fatty acid supplement, such as chicken fat, cod liver oil, salmon oil, fish oil, or safflower oil
- a bonemeal supplement: either natural bonemeal, finely ground eggshells, or a calcium lactate supplement
- a green-food supplement, such as blue-green algae, spirulina, or barley grass
- a health food blend, such as Springtime, Inc.'s Longevity or Tri-Natural Product's Missing Link

Supplements should be added as the food is served.

Food will remain good in the refrigerator for three to four days.

Variations:

- Use oatmeal instead of rice.
- Use turkey instead of chicken (although continue to use chicken broth).
- Use a pear instead of an apple.
- Use sweet potato instead of rice.
- Use spinach instead of green beans.

Beef and Squash . . . .

Dogs on a diet often feel like they are being deprived, just as people on a restricted diet sometimes feel. It's important that recipes for sedentary or overweight dogs taste good and provide the dog with a feeling of fullness, even if the food is still calorie restricted.

This recipe is about 900 calories, and all the dogs who did taste tests for us liked this food. This is one day's ration for an adult sedentary or overweight fifty-pound dog.

....

2 cups beef, muscle meat, cut into small pieces
1 cup summer squash, finely chopped
1 cup potato, russet or red, finely chopped
1/4 cup oat-bran flour
2 tablespoons tomato paste
Dash paprika

....

1. Put the potato on a paper plate or microwave-safe plate and cover with a wet paper towel. Cook until soft. (Potato can be steamed or baked if you prefer.)
2. Preheat oven to 350 degrees.
3. Put cooked potato, tomato paste, and oat flour in a bowl and mash together until well mixed.
4. Add the meat and squash and mix well.
5. Divide recipe in half and form each half into a meatloaf. Put in a mini loaf pan. Sprinkle a dash of paprika across the top of each meatloaf.
6. Bake for thirty minutes or until the meat is done.

Remove from oven and let cool. Each meatloaf is one meal. Refrigerate until serving time.

Suggested daily supplements include the following:

- a good-quality natural vitamin and mineral supplement
- a fatty acid supplement, such as chicken fat, cod liver oil, salmon oil, fish oil, or safflower oil
- a bonemeal supplement: either natural bonemeal, finely ground eggshells, or a calcium lactate supplement
- a green-food supplement, such as blue-green algae, spirulina, or barley grass

- a health food blend, such as Springtime, Inc.'s Longevity or Tri-Natural Product's Missing Link

Supplements should be added as the food is served.
Food will stay good in the refrigerator for three to four days.

Bison and Barley . . . .

This recipe is made with two rather unusual ingredients—barley and bison—which are very good for dogs showing signs of food allergies or food intolerances. However, it's also nutritious and about 1,200 calories, which is good for an active, fifty-pound adult dog.

2 cups raw bison
1 cup barley
1 tablespoon safflower oil

1. Put the barley on to cook according to package directions, and cook until well done. Drain off the excess water and set the cooked grains aside.
2. Cut the meat into bite-sized pieces. Brown until done but still tender. Add to the barley, scraping all the meat juices into the barley.
3. Turn off the heat and add the safflower oil, stirring until well mixed.

Divide the mixture into two serving portions and store in airtight containers. Refrigerate until time to serve.

Supplements should not be given at this time, as they could be causing allergic reactions, too. They should be added one at a time during the testing stage of the feeding.

Raw Beef, Greens, and Yams ....

This raw-food recipe contains about 1,200 calories. It is one day's worth of meals for the average forty- to fifty-pound dog, and contains no cereal grains or glutens.

....

> 2 cups beef, raw, ground, or muscle meat
> 1 cup fresh greens (spinach, collard greens,
>   broccoli florets)
> 1/2 cup yam, fresh
> 1/2 cup carrots, grated
> 2 tablespoons cod liver oil
> 1 tablespoon molasses
> 1 cup yogurt, plain, regular

....

1. Cut the beef into small bite-sized pieces and set aside.
2. Cut the greens into small pieces and place on a microwave-safe plate. Add the grated carrots. Cover with a wet paper towel and steam in the microwave, low heat, for about fifteen seconds. (Vegetables can be dipped into boiling water for about five seconds instead of microwaving if you prefer.)
3. Cut the yam into small pieces, cover with a wet paper towel, and steam for about a minute.
4. Add the greens, carrots, and yam to the meat. Add the cod liver oil and molasses and stir well, making sure the ingredients are well mixed so the dog can't leave the greens behind.

Divide into two meals. Add half of the yogurt to each meal when serving.

Refrigerate unused portion. Food will remain good in the refrigerator for a day or two; freeze unused meals.

Suggested supplements include the following:

- a good-quality natural vitamin and mineral supplement
- a bonemeal supplement: either natural bonemeal, finely ground eggshells, or a calcium lactate supplement
- a green-food supplement, such as blue-green algae, spirulina, or barley grass
- a health food blend, such as Springtime, Inc.'s Longevity or Tri-Natural Product's Missing Link

Supplements should be added as the food is served.
Variations:

- Use sweet potato in place of the yam.
- Use honey instead of the molasses.
- Use kefir instead of yogurt.

Turkey and Sweet Potato ....

This recipe makes one day's worth of meals for a forty- to fifty-pound dog of average activity levels. This recipe is 1,200 calories and contains no cereal grains or glutens.

2 cups turkey, ground or shredded muscle meat
2 eggs, chicken, hard-boiled, shelled
1 cup sweet potato, finely chopped
1/2 cup greens (spinach, broccoli, collard greens,
    Swiss chard, romaine lettuce)
2 teaspoons safflower oil
1/4 cup yogurt, plain, regular

1. If you're using leftover turkey, shred the meat into small pieces. If you're using fresh ground turkey, brown the meat.
2. Put the sweet potato on a microwave-safe plate or a paper plate and cover with a wet paper towel. Steam until the potato is tender. (Vegetables can be dipped into boiling water for about five seconds instead of microwaving if you prefer.)
3. Put the greens on a paper plate, cover with a wet paper towel, and steam for ten seconds.
4. Combine all the ingredients except the yogurt, making sure all of the ingredients are well mixed.

Divide into meals and store in the refrigerator in an airtight container.

When serving, add a portion of the yogurt to each meal.

Suggested daily supplements include the following:

- a good-quality natural vitamin and mineral supplement
- a bonemeal supplement: either natural bonemeal, finely ground eggshells, or a calcium lactate supplement
- a green-food supplement, such as blue-green algae, spirulina, or barley grass
- a health food blend, such as Springtime, Inc.'s Longevity or Tri-Natural Product's Missing Link

Supplements should be added as the food is served.

This food will be good in the refrigerator for two to three days.

Variations:

- Use chicken instead of turkey.
- Use cottage cheese instead of yogurt.

Antioxidant Special. . . . .

Dogs with arthritis or immune system deficiencies will benefit from a diet high in antioxidants.

2 cups tuna, raw, deboned
2 eggs, chicken, large
1/2 cup carrots, grated
1/4 cup spinach, fresh, finely grated
1/4 cup orange slices, fresh
1/4 cup orange juice
1/2 cup cheese, cheddar, grated

1. Preheat oven to 450 degrees.
2. Wrap the tuna in foil, place in baking pan, and bake until done, usually about ten minutes per inch of thickness of the fish.
3. When the fish is done, pull the pan out of the oven, unwrap the fish, and pull it apart (carefully, it's hot) until the fish is completely shredded.
4. Crack the two eggs over fish, add the carrots and spinach, and then stir the mixture, breaking the egg yolks and making sure everything is well mixed.
5. Sprinkle the cheddar cheese over the mixture.
6. Put back in the oven and bake for about ten minutes or until the eggs are thoroughly cooked and the cheese is melted.

Remove the pan from the oven and let the food cool. Divide into two or three meals (as many as your dog is used to eating in a day). Store in the refrigerator.

When serving, add a portion of the orange slices and pour a portion of the juice over the meat. Stir well.

Suggested daily supplements should include:

- a good-quality natural vitamin and mineral supplement, including zinc and antioxidants
- a fatty acid supplement, such as chicken fat, cod liver oil, salmon oil, fish oil, or safflower oil
- a bonemeal supplement: either natural bonemeal, finely ground eggshells, or a calcium lactate supplement
- a green-food supplement, such as blue-green algae, spirulina, or barley grass
- a health food blend, such as Springtime, Inc.'s Longevity or Tri-Natural Product's Missing Link

Supplements should be added as the food is served.

Food will remain good in the refrigerator for two to three days.

Canine Diabetic Recipe in the Slow Cooker . . . .

This recipe is very nutritious for your dog, yet also supplies a good deal of fiber and complex carbohydrates, both of which are important for the diabetic dog.

2 cups beef, ground, crumbled
$1/2$ cup red kidney beans, canned, low sodium
$1/2$ cup green beans, fresh or canned
$1/2$ cup greens (broccoli, collard greens, Swiss chard, or spinach)
1 cup oatmeal (not instant)
$1/4$ cup tomatoes, diced finely
$1/2$ cup goat cheese, crumbled

1. Brown the beef until the meat is thoroughly cooked.
2. Place the beef in the slow cooker, add the other ingredients (except the cheese), and cover with enough water to just cover them.
3. With the cooker on low, the ingredients can simmer all day.

Divide the cooked foods into servings, keeping the water and juices, too, and store in the refrigerator. When serving, sprinkle the goat cheese on top.

Suggested daily supplements include the following:

- a good-quality natural vitamin and mineral supplement
- a fatty acid supplement, such as chicken fat, cod liver oil, salmon oil, fish oil, or safflower oil
- a bonemeal supplement: either natural bonemeal, finely ground eggshells, or a calcium lactate supplement
- a nutritional yeast supplement
- a green-food supplement, such as blue-green algae, spirulina, or barley grass
- a health food blend, such as Springtime, Inc.'s Longevity or Tri-Natural Product's Missing Link

The herbal foods dandelion, parsley, and garlic are said to be good sources of nutrients for the diabetic pet.

Supplements should be added as the food is served.

Food will remain good in the refrigerator for two to three days.

Variations:

- Use grated summer squash instead of the kidney beans.
- Use grated zucchini instead of the greens.

Beef, Chicken, and Goat Cheese . . . .

This nutritious recipe supplies about 1,200 calories, is low sodium, and is good for most forty- to fifty-pound adult dogs with heart disease.

1 1/2 cups beef, ground, cooked
1/2 cup chicken, cooked, shredded
1/2 cup squash, any kind, precooked
1/2 cup potato, russet or red, precooked
1/4 cup goat cheese
1 tablespoon sesame oil

Preheat oven to 350 degrees.

1. Place the cooked ground beef in a bowl and break up any chunks. Add the shredded chicken, mix.
2. Cut the precooked squash and potato into small pieces (smaller than bite-sized for your dog is best). Add to the ground beef.
3. Add the cheese and oil, and then mix well.
4. Divide the mixture in half and shape each half into a small meatloaf. Put into a mini meatloaf pan (5½ by 3¼ by 1⅞ inches is a common size).
5. Bake for about thirty minutes or until a meat thermometer shows the meat is done inside (160 degrees).

Remove pans from oven, let cool, and store in the refrigerator. Each pan is one meal for a dog who is fed twice a day.

Suggested supplements include the following:

- a good-quality natural vitamin and mineral supplement

- a bonemeal supplement: either natural bonemeal, finely ground eggshells, or a calcium lactate supplement
- a nutritional yeast supplement
- a green-food supplement, such as blue-green algae, spirulina, or barley grass
- a health food blend, such as Springtime, Inc.'s Longevity or Tri-Natural Product's Missing Link

Supplements should be added as the food is served.
Food should remain good in the refrigerator for three to four days.
Variations:

- Substitute bison for the beef.
- Substitute venison or elk for the beef.
- Use duck, goose, or turkey instead of chicken.
- Use sweet potatoes or yams instead of russet potatoes.
- Use grated zucchini instead of butternut squash.
- Use mozzarella cheese (low or no sodium) instead of the goat cheese.

Turkey, Barley, and Kefir . . . .

This is a highly nutritious recipe that is low is salt and excellent for the aging dog's digestive system.

....

3 cups turkey, ground or shredded
$1/2$ cup barley, pearled
$1/2$ cup kefir

....

1. Put the turkey and barley in a saucepan and cover with water. Cook on high until the water is bubbling, then turn to low-medium and cook until the barley is soft.

Put the mixture, including any remaining water, in an airtight container in the refrigerator. Add a portion of the kefir to each serving.

Suggested supplements include the following:

- a good-quality natural vitamin and mineral supplement
- a fatty acid supplement, such as chicken fat, cod liver oil, salmon oil, fish oil, or safflower oil
- a bonemeal supplement: either natural bonemeal, finely ground eggshells, or a calcium lactate supplement
- a nutritional yeast supplement
- a green-food supplement, such as blue-green algae, spirulina, or barley grass
- a health food blend, such as Springtime, Inc.'s Longevity or Tri-Natural Product's Missing Link

Supplements should be added as the food is served.

Chicken, Eggs, and Goat Cheese . . . .

Eggs are the perfect food; they contain amino acids in excellent proportions and are easily digested. This is one day's meal for a fifty-pound dog of limited activity levels, or a dog with heart or kidney disease.

1 cup chicken, cooked, shredded
4 eggs, chicken, scrambled
1/2 cup zucchini, grated, steamed
1/2 cup potato, russet or red, precooked
1/4 cup goat cheese
1 tablespoon safflower oil

Preheat oven to 350 degrees.

1. Place the cooked shredded chicken in a bowl and make sure it's finely shredded.
2. Add the scrambled eggs to the chicken and mix.
3. Add the grated zucchini and cooked potato to the mixture. Add the cheese and oil, and then mix well.

Divide the mixture into servings and refrigerate.
Suggested supplements include the following:

- a good-quality natural vitamin and mineral supplement
- a bonemeal supplement: either natural bonemeal, finely ground eggshells, or a calcium lactate supplement
- a nutritional yeast supplement
- a green-food supplement, such as blue-green algae, spirulina, or barley grass
- a health food blend, such as Springtime, Inc.'s Longevity or Tri-Natural Product's Missing Link

Supplements should be added as the food is served.
Food should remain good in the refrigerator for three to four days.

Chicken and Cheese in the Slow Cooker . . . .

This recipe is very nutritious for your dog and contains protein sources that are more easily digested by the dog with liver disease. This is one day's meals for a fifty-pound dog.

2 cups turkey, ground, crumbled
1 cup greens (broccoli, collard greens,
Swiss chard, or spinach)

1 cup oatmeal (not instant)

¹/₄ cup tomatoes, diced finely

¹/₂ cup goat cheese, crumbled

··

1. Brown the turkey until the meat is thoroughly cooked.
2. Place the turkey in the slow cooker, add the other ingredients (except the cheese), and cover with enough water to just cover them.
3. With the cooker on low, the ingredients can simmer all day.

Divide the cooked foods into servings, keeping the water and juices, too, and store in the refrigerator. When serving, sprinkle the goat cheese on top.

Suggested daily supplements include the following:

- a good-quality natural vitamin and mineral supplement, including good, strong antioxidants
- a fatty acid supplement, such as chicken fat, cod liver oil, salmon oil, fish oil, or safflower oil
- a bonemeal supplement: either natural bonemeal, finely ground eggshells, or a calcium lactate supplement
- a nutritional yeast supplement
- a green-food supplement, such as blue-green algae, spirulina, or barley grass
- a health food blend, such as Springtime, Inc.'s Tonic Blend or Tri-Natural Product's Missing Link

The herbal foods milk thistle, licorice root, and red clover are excellent supplements for dogs with liver disease. Supplements should be added as the food is served.

Food will remain good in the refrigerator for two to three days.

Recipes for Cats

Low-Fat Oysters. . . . .

This tasty recipe has 330 calories and is a good recipe for a ten-pound indoor adult cat who needs limited calories and fat.

....

    1 cup oysters, fresh or canned, drained
    $^1/_2$ of a three-ounce can of tuna in water, drained
    1 egg, chicken, large, hard-boiled, crumbled
    2 tablespoons carrot, grated

....

1. Put all the ingredients in a food processor and liquefy until a thick paste. Add a tiny bit of the oyster or tuna water if needed for processing.
2. Put mixture in an airtight bowl and store in the refrigerator.

Divide into as many meals as your cat is used to eating. Suggested daily supplements include the following:

- a good-quality natural vitamin and mineral supplement
- a taurine supplement
- a bonemeal supplement: either natural bonemeal, finely ground eggshells, or a calcium lactate supplement
- a green-food supplement, such as blue-green algae, spirulina, or barley grass
- a health food blend, such as Tri-Natural Product's Missing Link for Cats

Supplements should be added as the food is served.

Chicken and Greens . . . .

Although cats are true carnivores, many do relish some occasional greens, and this recipe combines that need with the popular taste of chicken. Chuckles, an overweight Persian, enjoys this recipe so much his owner says he forgets it's a diet meal! This recipe has about 300 calories.

1 cup chicken, cooked, shredded finely
1/2 cup chicken broth
1 tablespoon wheatgrass, finely chopped, fresh
1 tablespoon spinach, finely chopped, fresh
4 tablespoons yogurt, plain, regular

1. Place the wheatgrass and spinach on a paper plate or a microwave-safe plate, and cover with a wet paper towel. Cook for ten seconds. (Vegetables can be dipped into boiling water for about five seconds instead of microwaving if you prefer.)
2. Mix the greens with the chicken and broth, mixing well.

Put in an airtight container and store in the refrigerator. Divide into as many servings as your cat is used to eating, and add a spoonful of yogurt to each serving.

Suggested daily supplements include the following:

- a good-quality natural vitamin and mineral supplement
- a taurine supplement
- a fatty acid supplement, such as chicken fat, cod liver oil, salmon oil, fish oil, or safflower oil
- a bonemeal supplement: either natural bonemeal, finely ground eggshells, or a calcium lactate supplement

- a green-food supplement, such as blue-green algae, spirulina, or barley grass
- a health food blend, such as Tri-Natural Product's Missing Link for Cats

Supplements should be added as the food is served.

Duck and Oatmeal Allergy Diet . . . .

This recipe provides about 325 calories, which is good for an average indoor ten- to twelve-pound cat.

....

> 2/3 cup duck, raw, chopped into
>   bite-sized pieces
> 1 egg, duck, hard-boiled, shell removed
> 2 tablespoons oatmeal, cooked (leftover from
>   breakfast is fine)
> 1 tablespoon cod liver oil

....

1. Cut the duck into strips for easier cooking, making sure no bones remain in the meat. Cook until done yet still tender. Cut or shred the chicken into very small bite-sized pieces for your cat.
2. While the chicken is cooking, break up the hard-boiled egg into a small bowl. Crumble it well.
3. Combine cooked duck, cod liver oil, and oatmeal in the bowl with the crumbled egg. Mix well.

Divide into two, three, four, or five meals (depending upon how many your cat is used to eating each day) and refrigerate the meals not being served immediately.

Supplements should be limited during this stage of the allergy testing. However, your cat should still receive a taurine supplement daily.

This food will remain good in the refrigerator for two to three days.

Raw Clams for Cats. . . . .

This recipe contains no cereal grains or grain glutens, and is about 350 calories, or one day's supply for a ten-pound indoor cat.

> 1 cup clams, raw
> 1/4 cup tuna, raw, cut into fine pieces
> 1 egg, chicken, hard-boiled, shelled, crumbled
> 1 teaspoon cod liver oil
> 2 tablespoons summer squash, grated
> 2 tablespoons wheatgrass, finely chopped

1. Put the clams, tuna, cod liver oil, and egg into a food processor and liquefy until a thick paste. Pour into a bowl.
2. Put the summer squash and wheatgrass on a paper plate, cover with a wet paper towel, and steam in the microwave for about ten seconds. (Vegetables can be dipped into boiling water for about five seconds instead of microwaving if you prefer.)
3. Add the grated summer squash and wheatgrass to the clam mixture and stir well.
4. Divide into servings.

Refrigerate in an airtight container until serving. Food will remain good for one to two days. Do not freeze leftovers; discard after two days.

Suggested daily supplements include the following:

- a good-quality natural vitamin and mineral supplement
- a taurine supplement
- a bonemeal supplement: either natural bonemeal, finely ground eggshells, or a calcium lactate supplement
- a green-food supplement, such as blue-green algae, spirulina, or barley grass
- a health food blend, such as Tri-Natural Product's Missing Link for Cats

Supplements should be added as the food is served.

Recipe for Diabetic Cats. . . . .

Diabetic cats should have fiber in their recipe, too, but many cats will not eat high-fiber foods. In this recipe, we'll try and sneak some in and see if the cats will accept it.

^{1}/2 cup chicken, cooked, ground or finely shredded
1 egg, chicken, hard-boiled, shelled
^{1}/2 cup greens, very finely chopped (wheatgrass, barley grass, spinach, romaine lettuce), lightly steamed
2 tablespoons tuna, canned in oil
1 tablespoon of the oil from the can of tuna

1. Mix all the ingredients gently, making sure the greens are well mixed in and everything is covered in tuna and tuna oil.

Divide into at least four servings. Store in an airtight container in the refrigerator. Food should remain good for two to three days.

Supplements recommended for diabetic cats include the following:

- a good-quality natural vitamin and mineral supplement
- a taurine supplement
- a bonemeal supplement: either natural bonemeal, finely ground eggshells, or a calcium lactate supplement
- a nutritional yeast supplement
- a teaspoon of yogurt
- a green-food supplement, such as blue-green algae, spirulina, or barley grass
- a health food blend, such as Tri-Natural Product's Missing Link for Cats

Chicken and Trout. . . . .

This recipe makes one day's food supply (about 375 calories) for an average indoor ten- to twelve-pound cat and is low in salt. This is also a very good recipe for cats with kidney or liver disease.

^{2}/3 cup chicken
^{1}/2 cup of trout (or another freshwater fish)
1 chicken egg, small, hard-boiled, remove the shell
2 tablespoons wheatgrass

1. Cut the chicken into strips for easier cooking, making sure no bones remain in the meat.
2. Cut the trout into strips and add to the chicken.
3. Cook until both meats are done yet still tender. Cut or shred the meats into very small bite-sized pieces for your cat.

4. While the chicken is cooking, break up the hard-boiled egg into a small bowl. Crumble it well.
5. Cut the wheatgrass into small pieces and place on a paper plate or microwave-safe plate. Cover with a damp paper towel and microwave for ten seconds. (Greens can be dipped into boiling water for about five seconds instead of microwaving if you prefer.)
6. Combine cooked chicken and trout with the wheatgrass and the crumbled egg. Mix well.

Divide into two, three, four, or five meals (depending upon how many your cat is used to eating each day) and refrigerate the meals not being served immediately.

Suggested daily supplements include the following:

- a good-quality natural vitamin and mineral supplement
- a taurine supplement
- a fatty acid supplement, such as chicken fat, cod liver oil, salmon oil, fish oil, or safflower oil.
- a bonemeal supplement: either natural bonemeal, finely ground eggshells, or a calcium lactate supplement
- a nutritional yeast supplement
- a teaspoon of yogurt
- a green-food supplement, such as blue-green algae, spirulina, or barley grass
- a health food blend, such as Tri-Natural Product's Missing Link for Cats

Supplements should be added as the food is served.

This food will remain good in the refrigerator for two to three days.

CHAPTER ELEVEN

Celebrations, Snacks, and Training Treats

Our dogs and cats have become a vital part of our lives; they are our companions and confidants. Dogs go for walks, jog, or swim with us, and provide us with security. Cats warm our laps and cuddle up in bed. As such a vital part of our lives, we like to share our celebrations with our pets, too, from birthday parties to holidays. And what's a better way to celebrate than with some special treats?

Cautions Regarding Treats

Since obesity is such a problem in dogs and cats today, before talking about treats, snacks, and celebrations, I really do need to throw in some cautions. Treats are not, and should not be, the bulk of your pet's diet; they need to be considered special.

Deb Eldredge, DVM, says, "Limit treats; they should never consist of more than 10 percent of your pet's daily diet." She also recommends reading labels, just as you read the label of your pet's food or ingredients for your pet's food. Avoid those treats that are full of sugar, fat, or are too high in cereal grains.

Treats don't have to be commercial treats, either, although there are some good commercial treats available. Many dogs enjoy carrots, slices of apple, berries, and bits of baked liver. Cats like bits of tuna, canned or fresh, as well as tiny pieces of chicken or cheese.

Other Cautions to Keep in Mind during the Holidays and Special Occasions

Some human treats aren't so good for dogs and cats. If you happen to receive a big box of chocolates, remember that it's not good for our furry friends.

During any holiday or special occasion, make sure that special foods are out of your pet's reach. Don't allow guests to share their special foods with your pet, either—that's how upset tummies happen!

If you enjoy having a Christmas tree, you may want to avoid using metallic tinsel on the tree; cats absolutely love it, but if a cat swallows that tinsel, it will cut his or her intestinal tract to ribbons. Also, if you have a puppy at home, put non-breakable ornaments on the tree within the puppy's reach. Or, better yet, save the glass ornaments for when the puppy is all grown up and well trained.

Commercial Treat Comparisons

SOME EXCELLENT DOG TREATS

Old Mother Hubbard makes a Wellness dog treat called Pure Rewards. The ingredients are beef, dried chicory root, cultured whey, sea salt, lecithin, garlic, and mixed tocopherols. In our taste tests, even the picky eaters ate these treats with enthusiasm.

Solid Gold makes Turkey Jerky Treats for Dogs, with the following ingredients: turkey, turkey meal, brown rice, cracked oats, tapioca meal, turkey liver, cane molasses, brown sugar, natural mesquite flavors, garlic, cinnamon, and rosemary. These treats were also eagerly eaten.

Natura Pet Products makes Evo Dog Treats, with the following ingredients: turkey, chicken, turkey meal, chicken meal, potato, herring meal, chicken fat, natural flavors, eggs, garlic, apples, carrots, tomatoes, cottage cheese, and dried chicory root. Although not as eagerly eaten as the first two treats, they were eaten by all our taste-testing dogs.

A LESS-THAN-GOOD TREAT

One dog bone-shaped treat that has been on the market for many years lists these as its ingredients: wheat flour, wheat bran, beef meal, beef bone meal, milk, wheat germ, beef fat, and vitamins and minerals.

EXPLANATION

With its three wheat ingredients, this is a wheat-based treat with beef. Wheat is a very common allergy-causing food for dogs.

Remedy for Fear

While many of us humans love celebrating New Year's Eve and the Fourth of July with lots of noise, these holidays can be difficult and frightening for those pets who are sensitive to sounds. Firecrackers and gunshots can send a pet scurrying for a hiding place. If your pet is sensitive to sound, make sure you keep him or her inside during all the noise; far too many pets try to escape from their yards in fear.

A homeopathic remedy that works for many pets is called Rescue Remedy, made by Bach Flower Remedies. It contains rock rose, star of Bethlehem, cherry plum, and crab apple. The drops can be mixed in the pet's water or dropped into the mouth. Rescue Remedy can be found at pet stores that carry herbal remedies or health food stores.

Recipes for Dogs

New Year's Good Luck ....

This recipe is a special treat, and although it is very nutritious, it is not a balanced daily diet.

2 cups beef, ground, crumbled
1 cup black-eyed peas
$1/2$ cup wild or brown rice
$1/4$ cup tomatoes, finely diced
$1/2$ cup goat cheese, crumbled

1. Soak the peas in water overnight. Drain off the water, and put in the slow cooker with the heat off.
2. Brown the ground beef. When the meat is done, transfer to the slow cooker, adding the meat juices, too.
3. Place the other ingredients in the slow cooker also, and add just enough water to cover the ingredients.
4. Turn the heat to high until the ingredients are bubbling, then turn to low. Let cook for five to six hours.

When done, let the foods cool before serving. Serve a spoonful as a special treat (and for good luck!), or add a heaping spoonful to your pet's regular food and supplements. Refrigerate remaining foods for three to four days. Freeze any excess food.

Valentine Treats. . . . .

I think most dog owners enjoy sharing the holidays with their pets, including Valentine's Day. This recipe creates some very special treats. It's fun to make a batch of these and take them to the dog park or training yard to share with friends. This is a treat, not a balanced meal or diet.

2 cans of refrigerated pizza dough
1 cup chicken, cooked, chopped in small pieces
1/2 cup chicken broth

1. Preheat oven to 350 degrees.
2. Take one can of the pizza dough and remove from the can. Place it on a lightly floured bread board, and carefully (so you don't rip the dough) stretch it flat and thin.
3. Use a heart-shaped cookie cutter to cut out as many heart shapes as you can from the dough. Place the cookies on a greased cookie sheet.

4. Place a bit of chicken on each cookie.
5. Using the second can of dough, repeat the first and second steps, except place the heart shapes on top of the piece of chicken, so you are creating a cookie-dough sandwich.
6. Seal the edges of each cookie by pressing the edges together with the tines of a fork.
7. Using a pastry brush or a new, clean paintbrush, gently brush each cookie top with chicken broth.
8. Bake the cookies for fifteen minutes or until golden brown.

Remove from oven and let cool. Store in an airtight container in the refrigerator.

Halloween Treats. . . . .

All the dogs who taste tested our treats enjoyed this one. It's tasty and timely.

. . . .

> 1 can refrigerated crescent dough
> ¹/₂ cup pumpkin, canned

. . . .

1. Preheat oven to 350 degrees.
2. Open the can of dough, and carefully spread it out on a lightly floured bread board. Separate each crescent triangle.
3. Leave the triangles intact and place them flat on the bread board.
4. Place a small dab of pumpkin on each triangle.
5. Fold the triangles, using the tines of a fork to seal the edges, and then place them on a greased cookie sheet.
6. Bake for seven to nine minutes or until golden brown.

Let the treats cool. Store in an airtight container in the refrigerator.

Thanksgiving Turkey and Sweet Potato . . . .

This recipe can be made with the same ingredients you're using to make your own Thanksgiving dinner. Just set aside a little food and make a special treat to be added to your dog's daily diet.

    1 cup turkey, cooked, finely chopped
    1 cup sweet potato, cooked, chopped
    2 eggs, large, hard-boiled, shelled

1. Place all three ingredients in a food processor and liquefy until a thick paste. If the food is too thick, add just enough water for processing.

Give a small dog just a teaspoon or two on his or her normal food. Larger dogs can have a heaping tablespoon.
Refrigerate extra until the next meal.

Christmas Canes . . . .

Do you have friends who have dogs? This is an easy recipe that creates colorful, edible canes for dogs. Put two or three in a small gift bag for each friend's dog and tie with a holiday ribbon.

    1 can refrigerated pizza dough
    ¹/₄ cup flour
    1 tablespoon dry beef bullion
    Red food coloring (natural food coloring from the
        health-food store is great)

1. Preheat oven to 350 degrees.
2. Put the flour and bullion on a bread board, mixing the two together.
3. Take the dough out of the package and spread it out on the floured bread board. Stretch it until it's about a quarter inch thick, taking care not to rip the dough.
4. Divide the dough in half lengthwise, and set one piece aside.
5. Drop several drops of red food coloring on the remaining piece of dough. Spread the drops around on the dough; you may want to wear gloves. (The entire piece doesn't have to be dark red; streaks and spots are fun.)
6. Using a sharp knife, cut that piece of dough into long strips that are between a quarter and a half inch wide. Set these aside.
7. Take the other piece of dough and spread it out; this will be the white pieces. Cut it into strips also.
8. Take a piece of red dough and a piece of white dough and twist the two together, then hook the top third of the strips, creating a candy cane. Place on a greased cookie sheet.
9. Continue with the rest of the dough.
10. Bake for about ten minutes or until the bottoms are golden brown.

Remove from oven and let cool. To make crisper canes, turn the oven off but don't remove the cookie sheet from the oven. Let the cookies harden in the oven as it cools down. While the oven is still hot, watch to make sure they don't get too brown.

Store in an airtight container until you package them for gifts.

Beef Liver Treats . . . .

All the dogs who did taste tests for us, from Great Danes to toy poodles, liked these liver treats.

> 1 pound beef liver, chopped finely
> 1 cup flaxseed meal, finely ground
> 2 eggs, large
> 1/4 cup safflower oil
> 1/4 cup warm water
> 1 cup flaxseed meal for coating treats

1. Preheat oven to 350 degrees.
2. Mix together all the ingredients except the second cup of flaxseed meal, making sure the pieces of the liver are well coated. The dough will be stiff.
3. For larger dogs, form the dough into teaspoon-sized balls, and then roll the balls in the remaining flaxseed meal.
4. For smaller dogs, form the dough into smaller bite-sized balls, and roll the balls in the remaining flaxseed meal.
5. Place the balls on a greased cookie sheet.
6. The larger dog treats should bake for ten to fifteen minutes or until the bottoms are golden brown. The small dog treats will need less time; check them after five minutes. Don't let the bottoms of the treats scorch.

Remove from the oven, let cool thoroughly, and store in an airtight container in the refrigerator.

Treats should remain good for a week or so in the refrigerator.

Chicken and Yams. . . . .

This recipe for dog treats will appeal to the pickiest eaters. It is healthy and tasty.

1 1/4 cups chicken, cooked, shredded into small pieces
1/2 cup yams, cooked, cut into pieces no longer than a half inch
2 cups oat flour
1 cup goat's milk, canned or fresh
1/2 teaspoon salt
1/2 teaspoon baking powder
2 eggs, chicken, large

1. Preheat the oven to 350 degrees.
2. Mix all the ingredients, making sure the pieces of chicken are well coated.
3. Drop by teaspoonful onto a greased cookie sheet.
4. Bake for twelve to fifteen minutes or until the bottoms are golden brown.

Remove from oven, let cool, and then store in an airtight container in the refrigerator.

Crunchy Biscuit Bones . . . .

We can't talk about dog treats without having a recipe for crunchy dog-biscuit bones. Here's a popular recipe.

3 1/2 cups oat flour
1/3 cup beef or chicken bullion
1/2 teaspoon baking powder

^{1}/2 teaspoon salt

1 tablespoon molasses, dark

2 eggs, chicken, large

1 cup warm water

1 cup oat flour for the bread board

^{1}/2 cup flaxseed meal for the cutting board

1. Preheat oven to 350 degrees.
2. Mix the first four ingredients in a mixing bowl.
3. Slowly add the molasses, eggs, and water. The dough should be stiff.
4. Use your hands to mix and knead the dough until it is well mixed and easy to handle.
5. Put the oat flour and flaxseed meal on the bread board and mix. Put the dough on the board, and roll out to three-eighths to one-half inch thick; thick is fine.
6. Using a dog bone–shaped cookie cutter, cut out the cookies, and place them on a greased cookie sheet.

Bake until the bottoms of the cookies are golden brown; the time will vary depending upon the thickness of the dough and the size of your dog-bone cookie cutter.

When all the cookies are done, turn the oven off, put all the cookies back on to one cookie sheet, and return it to the oven. Let them get crunchier as the oven cools; you can even leave them there overnight.

Store in an airtight container.

Just Because Snack Rolls. . . . .

These treats are a "just because" treat. Your dog deserves them once in a while for no reason whatsoever!

....

4 pieces of lasagna pasta, cooked and soft
1/2 cup meat, leftovers are great
1/4 cup cheese, grated

....

1. Place the lasagna pasta flat on a bread board.
2. Place small bits of the meat on the pasta, spreading it out.
3. Sprinkle the grated cheese over the meat.
4. Starting at the end of one piece of pasta, roll up the pasta with the meat and cheese inside. Place on a paper plate and repeat with the other pieces of pasta.
5. Place a damp paper towel over the rolls and microwave until the cheese is melted (forty to sixty seconds).
6. For small dogs, slice the rolls across one end, and each slice can be a treat. For larger dogs, divide the rolls in half.

Wrap each roll in clear plastic wrap and store in the refrigerator. Treats should remain good for a few days, depending upon how old the leftovers were.

Beef Liver Training Treats ....

I hate to cook liver; I can't stand the smell. I do break down and make this recipe, though, every once in a while, because my dogs absolutely love it! These make wonderful training treats.

....

2 tablespoons dry active yeast
1/4 cup warm water
2 1/2 cups oat flour
1 cup nonfat dry milk
1/4 cup safflower oil
2 tablespoons molasses, dark

1 egg, chicken, large
8 ounces of beef liver, finely chopped, cooked

1. Preheat oven to 350 degrees.
2. Dissolve the yeast in the warm water and let sit for a few minutes.
3. Mix the flour and dry milk in a mixing bowl. Add the yeast and water, the oil, molasses, and egg. Mix well.
4. Add the liver to the mixture and mix well; the dough will be stiff, so you may want to use your hands to mix and knead the dough.
5. Drop by training-treat size (a pea size for a small dog and a gumdrop size for a large dog) to a greased cookie sheet.
6. Bake until the bottoms are golden brown, maybe four to five minutes for the smallest size and twenty minutes for larger treats.

Remove from the oven and let cool. Store in an airtight container in the refrigerator where treats should remain good for a week.

Recipes for Cats

New Year's Good Luck . . . .

This recipe for cats is a special treat and very nutritious but is not a balanced daily diet.

2 cups beef, ground, crumbled
1/4 cup black-eyed peas
1/2 cup wild or brown rice

¹/4 cup tomatoes, finely diced
¹/2 cup goat cheese, crumbled

1. Soak the peas in water overnight. Drain off the water, and put in the slow cooker with the heat off.
2. Brown the ground beef. When the meat is done, transfer to a slow cooker, adding the meat juices, too.
3. Place the other ingredients in the slow cooker also, and add just enough water to cover the ingredients.
4. Turn the heat to high until the ingredients are bubbling, then turn to low. Let cook for five to six hours.

When done, let the foods cool before serving. Serve a spoonful as a special treat (and for good luck!), or add a heaping spoonful to your pet's regular food and supplements. Refrigerate remaining food for three to four days. Freeze any excess food.

Dried Catnip . . . .

You will need a food dehydrator and several catnip plants for this recipe.

Many cats enjoy the mild stimulating effects of catnip, and their owners definitely enjoy watching their cats play with this herb. Even the most dignified of cats will act like a silly kitten when rolling in catnip! You can find catnip plants at any plant nursery that sells herbs and even many hardware or discount-store nurseries.

Plant the catnip in a sunny spot, in the ground or in a medium-sized pot. Use as few chemicals as possible (herbicides, fertilizers, or insecticides), and definitely don't use any within two weeks of picking any blossoms.

Within a couple of months the plant should blossom; this is the time to trim it back so it can regrow. The plant can be gently trimmed throughout the growing season, snipping off the tops of each flowering stem (six inches or so, depending on how tall your plant is). The trimmings can be given to your cat fresh, but you will also want to dry some of the trimmings to keep for use after the plant has gone by.

Place the entire stem on the dehydrator racks. Do not pick the flowers or leaves off the stems. Spread the stems out so they are not piled on top of each other. Dry for two to three hours, or until the thickest leaf and stem is completely dry.

Once dry, pick the leaves and flowers off the stems. Place them in an airtight container, slightly crumpling them as you do. Mix the leaves and flowers in the same bag.

You can use this dried catnip in a variety of ways. Take your cat's favorite soft toy and stuff part of it with the catnip, or store the toy in an airtight container with catnip for a few days so it picks up the scent. If you have gotten a new scratching post for your cat, rub some of the catnip over the post where you want your cat to scratch. You can even sprinkle a tiny bit of the catnip over your cat's food.

Halloween Treats. . . . .

Cats will enjoy this treat; it's tasty and timely.

. . . .

     1 can refrigerated crescent dough
     1/2 cup pumpkin, canned

. . . .

1. Preheat oven to 350 degrees.
2. Open the can of dough, and carefully spread it out on a lightly floured bread board. Separate each crescent triangle.

3. Cut each triangle into three additional triangles.
4. Place a small dab of pumpkin on each triangle.
5. Fold the triangles, using the tines of a fork to seal the edges, and then place them on a greased cookie sheet.
6. Bake for seven to nine minutes or until golden brown.

Let the treats cool. Store in an airtight container in the refrigerator.

Most cats enjoy pureed pumpkin but to introduce a finicky cat to these treats, break the treat open and encourage the cat to sniff and taste the pumpkin.

Turkey and Sweet Potato . . . .

This recipe can be made with the same ingredients you're using to make your own Thanksgiving dinner. Just set aside a little food and make a special treat to be added to your pet's daily diet.

1 cup turkey, cooked, finely chopped
1 cup sweet potato, cooked, chopped
2 eggs, large, hard-boiled, shelled

1. Place all three ingredients in a food processor and liquefy until it's a thick paste. If the food is too thick, add just enough water for processing.

Give a cat just a teaspoon or two on his or her normal food. Refrigerate extra until the next meals.

Beef Liver Treats . . . .

The only cats who turned up their noses at this treat were those who were used to eating home-cooked or raw foods; they didn't care for the crispy texture. The cats who normally ate kibble foods loved these treats.

1 pound beef liver, chopped finely
1 cup flaxseed meal, finely ground
2 eggs, large
^{1}/4 cup safflower oil
^{1}/4 cup warm water
1 cup flaxseed meal for coating treats

1. Preheat oven to 350 degrees.
2. Mix together all the ingredients except the second cup of flaxseed meal, making sure the pieces of the liver are well coated. The dough will be stiff.
3. Form the dough into bite-sized balls, and roll the balls in the remaining flaxseed meal.
4. Place the balls on a greased cookie sheet.
5. The treats will need to bake about five to seven minutes. Don't let the bottoms of the treats scorch.

Remove from the oven, let cool thoroughly, and store in an airtight container in the refrigerator.

Treats should remain good for a week or so in the refrigerator.

A Finicky-Feline Favorite . . . .

This recipe can be made with several variations, so make sure to look at those at the end of the recipe. With variations, this can be made to suit any cat's tastes, even the pickiest.

....

1 slice roast beef, cooked, very thinly sliced
   (as sliced for lunch meat)
1 tablespoon cream cheese, soft, plain
1 tablespoon wheatgrass, finely chopped

....

1. Place the piece of lunch meat on the cutting board.
2. Gently, so you don't rip the meat, spread the cream cheese on the meat.
3. Sprinkle the chopped wheatgrass on the cream cheese.
4. Starting at one side, roll up the roast beef so the cream cheese is inside. When you have one rolled, and all the cream cheese is inside, gently press on the roll so it remains rolled up.
5. Starting at one end, slice off quarter-inch slices. Each slice is one cat treat.

Wrap the unused portion of the roll in a clear plastic wrap and store in the refrigerator. It will remain good for a few days.

Variations:

- Use a soft cheddar cheese instead of cream cheese.
- Use a thin slice of swiss cheese instead of the cream cheese.
- Use a thin slice of turkey instead of the roast beef.
- Use a thin slice of raw fish (minus the bones) instead of the roast beef.

Tuna Training Treats . . . .

Most cats love tuna; sometimes the problem is getting them to eat something other than tuna! This recipe uses the feline love of tuna to create some tasty training treats.

1 six-ounce can of tuna in oil, undrained
1 tablespoon yogurt, regular, plain
$1/2$ cup bread crumbs, unseasoned, plain

1. Put the tuna, the oil from the tuna can, and the yogurt in a food processor and blend until it's a thick paste. Scrape into a mixing bowl.
2. Add the bread crumbs and mix well.
3. Put in an airtight container in the refrigerator for at least an hour, until the bread crumbs have absorbed some moisture.

During training, serve a tiny bit on the end of a popsicle stick or a small spoon.

Store in the refrigerator for up to a week.

Appendix: Food Values

Apple, raw, chopped, 1 cup
  Calories 74
  Protein (grams) 0
  Carbohydrates 19
  Fat 0.5
  Sodium 0
  Fiber 3
Apple, raw, 1 medium
  Calories 81
  Protein (grams) 0
  Carbohydrates 21
  Fat 0.5
  Sodium 0
  Fiber 4
Applesauce, unsweetened,
  ½ cup
  Calories 58
  Protein (grams) 0
  Carbohydrates 15

  Fat 0
  Sodium 0
  Fiber 1
Bacon (pork), cooked,
  3 slices
  Calories 109
  Protein (grams) 6
  Carbohydrates 0
  Fat 9
  Sodium 300 (can vary)
  Fiber 0
Barley, pearled, cooked,
  1 cup
  Calories 193
  Protein (grams) 4
  Carbohydrates 44
  Fat 0.7
  Sodium 5
  Fiber 6

**Beans, red kidney, canned,
½ cup**
Calories 120
Protein (grams) 7
Carbohydrates 23
Fat 1
Sodium 400
Fiber 0
**Beef, ground, cooked,
1 cup (equals 5 ounces)**
Calories 370
Protein (grams) 40
Carbohydrates 0
Fat 4
Sodium 115
Fiber 0
Bison, 1 cup
Calories 150
Protein (grams) 30
Carbohydrates 0
Fat 2.5
Sodium 60
Fiber 0
Blueberries, frozen, 1 cup
Calories 79
Protein (grams) 1
Carbohydrates 19
Fat 1
Sodium 2
Fiber 4
**Broccoli, fresh, florets,
1 cup**
Calories 20
Protein (grams) 2
Carbohydrates 4

Fat 0.2
Sodium 19
Fiber 4
**Broccoli, fresh, stems and
florets, 1 cup**
Calories 25
Protein (grams) 3
Carbohydrates 5
Fat 0.3
Sodium 24
Fiber 3
**Carrots, fresh grated,
1 cup**
Calories 47
Protein (grams) 1
Carbohydrates 11
Fat 0.2
Sodium 39
Fiber 3
**Celery, 1 stalk about
8 inches long**
Calories 6
Protein (grams) 0
Carbohydrates 1
Fat 0
Sodium 1
Fiber 1
**Cheese, cheddar, shredded,
½ cup**
Calories 200
Protein (grams) 14
Carbohydrates 2
Fat 16
Sodium 320
Fiber 0

**Cheese, cottage, regular,
½ cup**
  Calories 120
  Protein (grams) 14
  Carbohydrates 4
  Fat 5
  Sodium 420
  Fiber 0
**Cheese, cream, regular,
2 tablespoons**
  Calories 70
  Protein (grams) 3
  Carbohydrates 2
  Fat 5
  Sodium 150
  Fiber 0
Cheese, feta, 1 ounce
  Calories 75
  Protein (grams) 4
  Carbohydrates 1
  Fat 6
  Sodium 316
  Fiber 0
**Cheese, goat, semisoft,
1 ounce**
  Calories 103
  Protein (grams) 6
  Carbohydrates 1
  Fat 9
  Sodium 146
  Fiber 0
**Cheese, mozzarella,
½ cup**
  Calories 158
  Protein (grams) 15

  Carbohydrates 2
  Fat 10
  Sodium 300
  Fiber 0
**Chicken, cooked, 1 cup
(5 ounces)**
  Calories 250
  Protein (grams) 43
  Carbohydrates 0
  Fat 7
  Sodium 108
  Fiber 0
**Chicken broth, regular,
1 cup**
  Calories 38
  Protein (grams) 5
  Carbohydrates 1
  Fat 1.5
  Sodium 470
  Fiber 0
Clam, mixed species, 1 large
  Calories 15
  Protein (grams) 3
  Carbohydrates 1
  Fat 0
  Sodium 11
  Fiber 0
Deer, see Venison
Egg, chicken, large
  Calories 86
  Protein (grams) 7
  Carbohydrates 1
  Fat 6
  Sodium 73
  Fiber 0

Egg, duck
  Calories 130
  Protein (grams) 9
  Carbohydrates 1
  Fat 10
  Sodium 102
  Fiber 0
Egg, goose
  Calories 267
  Protein (grams) 20
  Carbohydrates 2
  Fat 20
  Sodium 199
  Fiber 0
Egg, quail
  Calories 14
  Protein (grams) 2
  Carbohydrates 0
  Fat 1
  Sodium 13
  Fiber 0
Egg, turkey
  Calories 135
  Protein (grams) 11
  Carbohydrates 1
  Fat 10
  Sodium 120
  Fiber 0
Flaxseeds, unground, ¼ cup
  Calories 190
  Protein (grams) 8
  Carbohydrates 14
  Fat 14
  Sodium 14
  Fiber 11

Flour, barley, 1 cup
  Calories 510
  Protein (grams) 16
  Carbohydrates 110
  Fat 3
  Sodium 6
  Fiber 15
Flour, oat bran, 1 cup
  Calories 110
  Protein (grams) 3
  Carbohydrates 24
  Fat 1
  Sodium 3
  Fiber 3
Flour, potato, 1 cup
  Calories 570
  Protein (grams) 11
  Carbohydrates 133
  Fat 0.5
  Sodium 88
  Fiber 10
Flour, rice, 1 cup
  Calories 575
  Protein (grams) 9
  Carbohydrates 127
  Fat 2
  Sodium 0
  Fiber 4
Flour, wheat, bleached, all-purpose, 1 cup
  Calories 400
  Protein (grams) 11
  Carbohydrates 87
  Fat 1
  Sodium 0
  Fiber 0

Garlic oil, 1 tablespoon
Calories 120
Protein (grams) 0
Carbohydrates 0
Fat 14
Sodium 0
Fiber 0

Gelatin, Knox, unflavored, 1 packet
Calories 20
Protein (grams) 8
Carbohydrates 0
Fat 0
Sodium 0
Fiber 0

Goat milk, canned, evaporated, ½ cup
Calories 150
Protein (grams) 10
Carbohydrates 12
Fat 8
Sodium 120
Fiber 0

Green beans, fresh, raw, ½ cup
Calories 17
Protein (grams) 1
Carbohydrates 4
Fat 0.1
Sodium 7
Fiber 4

Green beans, string, canned, ½ cup
Calories 20
Protein (grams) 1

Carbohydrates 5
Fat 0
Sodium 350
Fiber 0

Honey, 1 tablespoon
Calories 60
Protein (grams) 0
Carbohydrates 16
Fat 0
Sodium 0
Fiber 0

Lamb, ground, cooked, 1 cup (4 ounces)
Calories 385
Protein (grams) 20
Carbohydrates 0
Fat 30
Sodium 120
Fiber 0

Millet, pearled, cooked, ½ cup
Calories 143
Protein (grams) 5
Carbohydrates 29
Fat 2
Sodium 2
Fiber 2

Molasses, dark, 1 tablespoon
Calories 47
Protein (grams) 0
Carbohydrates 12
Fat 0
Sodium 11
Fiber 0

**Oatmeal, old-fashioned,
    uncooked, 1 cup**
   Calories 300
   Protein (grams) 12
   Carbohydrates 60
   Fat 6
   Sodium 3
   Fiber 10

Oil, garlic, 1 tablespoon
   Calories 120
   Protein (grams) 0
   Carbohydrates 0
   Fat 14
   Sodium 0
   Fiber 0

Oil, safflower, 1 tablespoon
   Calories 120
   Protein (grams) 0
   Carbohydrates 0
   Fat 14
   Sodium 0
   Fiber 0

Oil, sesame, 1 tablespoon
   Calories 120
   Protein (grams) 0
   Carbohydrates 0
   Fat 14
   Sodium 0
   Fiber 0

**Oil, vegetable, salad/cooking,
    1 tablespoon**
   Calories 120
   Protein (grams) 0
   Carbohydrates 0
   Fat 13

   Sodium 0
   Fiber 0

Oysters, wild, raw, 1 cup
   Calories 169
   Protein (grams) 17
   Carbohydrates 10
   Fat 6
   Sodium 500
   Fiber 7

Parsley, fresh, raw, ¼ cup
   Calories 5
   Protein (grams) 0.5
   Carbohydrates 1
   Fat 0
   Sodium 8
   Fiber 0.5

Pasta, lasagna, 1 slice
   Calories 250
   Protein (grams) 9
   Carbohydrates 47
   Fat 3
   Sodium 15
   Fiber 2

Pasta, spiral, cooked, 1 cup
   Calories 200
   Protein (grams) 7
   Carbohydrates 40
   Fat 1
   Sodium 1
   Fiber 2

**Peanut butter, chunky,
    1 cup**
   Calories 1,520
   Protein (grams) 62
   Carbohydrates 56

Fat 128
Sodium 1,254
Fiber 17

**Peanut butter, chunky,
1 tablespoon**
Calories 94
Protein (grams) 4
Carbohydrates 4
Fat 8
Sodium 78
Fiber 1

**Popcorn, butter-flavor,
low-salt, microwave,
popped, 1 cup**
Calories 33
Protein (grams) 1
Carbohydrates 4
Fat 1
Sodium 22
Fiber 0

**Potato, russet, baked,
1/2 cup**
Calories 57
Protein (grams) 1
Carbohydrates 13
Fat 0.1
Sodium 3
Fiber 1

Rabbit, meat, 1 cup
Calories 200
Protein (grams) 30
Carbohydrates 0
Fat 10
Sodium 60
Fiber 0

**Rice, white, instant, cooked,
1 cup**
Calories 162
Protein (grams) 3
Carbohydrates 35
Fat 0.3
Sodium 5
Fiber 1

**Rice, wild, cooked,
1 cup**
Calories 166
Protein (grams) 7
Carbohydrates 35
Fat 0.6
Sodium 5
Fiber 3

**Salmon, canned in oil,
3 1/4-ounce can**
Calories 110
Protein (grams) 16
Carbohydrates 1
Fat 4
Sodium 420
Fiber 0

Sesame oil, 1 tablespoon
Calories 120
Protein (grams) 0
Carbohydrates 0
Fat 14
Sodium 0
Fiber 0

Spinach, fresh, raw, 1/2 cup
Calories 4
Protein (grams) 1
Carbohydrates 1

Fat 0
Sodium 12
Fiber 1

**Squash, acorn, fresh, boiled,
1 cup**
Calories 56
Protein (grams) 1
Carbohydrates 15
Fat 1
Sodium 4
Fiber 2

**Squash, butternut, fresh,
boiled, 1 cup**
Calories 63
Protein (grams) 1
Carbohydrates 16
Fat 0.5
Sodium 6
Fiber 1

**Squash, spaghetti, fresh,
boiled, 1 cup**
Calories 31
Protein (grams) 1
Carbohydrates 7
Fat 0.5
Sodium 17
Fiber 1

**Sweet potato, fresh, boiled,
1 cup**
Calories 344
Protein (grams) 5
Carbohydrates 80
Fat 1
Sodium 44
Fiber 6

**Tomato paste, canned, no salt
added, 1 tablespoon**
Calories 18
Protein (grams) 1
Carbohydrates 4
Fat 0.1
Sodium 20
Fiber 1

**Tuna, canned in oil,
3-ounce can**
Calories 160
Protein (grams) 23
Carbohydrates 0
Fat 7
Sodium 330
Fiber 0

**Tuna, canned in water,
3-ounce can**
Calories 99
Protein (grams) 22
Carbohydrates 0
Fat 1
Sodium 280
Fiber 0

Tuna, raw, fresh, 1 cup
Calories 230
Protein (grams) 35
Carbohydrates 0
Fat 5
Sodium 60
Fiber 0

**Turkey, cooked, ground or
shredded, 1 cup (5 ounces)**
Calories 262
Protein (grams) 40

Carbohydrates 0
Fat 4
Sodium 100
Fiber 0
**Vegetable oil, salad/cooking,
1 tablespoon**
Calories 120
Protein (grams) 0
Carbohydrates 0
Fat 13
Sodium 0
Fiber 0
**Venison (deer), raw,
1 cup**
Calories 160
Protein (grams) 60
Carbohydrates 0
Fat 5
Sodium 60
Fiber 0
Wheatgrass, fresh, 1 cup
Calories 214
Protein (grams) 8
Carbohydrates 46

Fat 1
Sodium 17
Fiber 1
Yam, fresh, raw, 1 cup
Calories 177
Protein (grams) 2
Carbohydrates 42
Fat 0.5
Sodium 10
Fiber 6
Yogurt, plain, 1 cup
Calories 200
Protein (grams) 12
Carbohydrates 16
Fat 9
Sodium 140
Fiber 0
Zucchini, fresh, 1 large
Calories 52
Protein (grams) 4
Carbohydrates 11
Fat 1
Sodium 32
Fiber 3

Bibliography

Researching and writing about a subject as complex as canine and feline nutrition is difficult. It's much like raising a child; everyone has a different opinion, and everyone is convinced he or she is right and knows best. If you have questions or doubts, feel free to do some research yourself!

Books

Anderson, Jean, MS, and Barbara Deskins, PhD, RD, *The Nutrition Bible,* William Morrow and Company, 1995.

Bonham, Margaret, and James M. Wingert, DVM, *The Complete Idiot's Guide to Dog Health and Nutrition,* Alpha Books, 2003.

The Complete Book of Foods, Avery, 2001.

Dunne, Lavon J., *Nutrition Almanac,* McGraw-Hill, 2002.

Goldstein, Robert, VMD, and Susan J. Goldstein, *The Goldsteins' Wellness and Longevity Program,* TFH Publications, 2005.

Jacobs, Jocelynn, DVM, *Performance Dog Nutrition,* Sno Shire Publications, 2005.

Lonsdale, Tom, *Work Wonders*, Rivetco P/L, 2005.

Messonnier, Shawn, DVM, *Natural Health Bible for Dogs & Cats*, Prima Publishing, 2001.

Null, Gary, PhD, *The Complete Encyclopedia of Natural Healing*, Bottom Line Books, 2006.

Palika, Liz, *The Ultimate Cat Treat Cookbook*, Howell Book House, 2006.

Palika, Liz, *The Ultimate Dog Treat Cookbook*, Howell Book House, 2005.

Shojai, Amy D., *Complete Care for Your Aging Dog*, New American Library, 2003.

Thornton, Kim Campbell, and Debra Eldredge, DVM, *The Everything Dog Health Book*, Adams Media, 2005.

Volhard, Wendy, and Kerry Brown, DVM, *Holistic Guide for a Healthy Dog*, Howell Book House, 2000.

Weiskopf, Joan, *Pet Food Nation*, Collins, 2007.

Internet, Newspaper, and Magazine Articles

Animal Protection Institute, "What's Really in Pet Food," *www.api4animals.org*.

ASPCA, "List of Top 10 Hazards," March 5, 2007, *www.aspca.org/site/PageServer?pagename=press_030507*.

Belfield, Wendell O., DVM, "Food Not Fit for a Pet," *Nexus*, December 1996.

Body Biology, "More Than Just Beneficial Bacteria," *www.kefir.net*.

Bren, Linda, "Pet Food: The Lowdown on Labels," *FDA Veterinarian*, July/August 2001.

Centers for Disease Control and Prevention, "Salmonellosis," November 4, 2006, *www.cdc.gov/ncidod/dbmd/diseaseinfo/salmonellosis_g.htm*.

Dawson, Faith, "Bites of Information," *Union-Tribune*, Tuesday, May 29, 2007.

Degner, Daniel, DVM, "Megacolon," Vet Surgery Central Inc., *www.vetsurgerycentral.com*.

Donoghue, Susan, DVM, "Nutrition: Feeding Our Dogs," *AKC Gazette*, May 2007, and "Nutrition: High Fat, Healthy Fuel," *AKC Gazette*, July 2007.

Dunn, T. J., Jr., DVM, "Omega Fatty Acids and Your Dog and Cat," Pet Center.com, *www.thepetcenter.com*.

Dyverson, Dave, AAFCO Pet Food Committee, "Questions and Answers Concerning Pet Food Regulation," June 26, 2007.

Editors at *Scientific American*, "Opinion: Take Nutrition Claims with a Grain of Salt," *Scientific American*, September 2007, and "News Scan: Protein Pretense," August 2007.

Eldredge, Debra, DVM, "Health Matters: OCD," *Dogs in Review*, Febrary/March 2007.

Fischetti, Mark, "Is Your Food Contaminated?" *Scientific American*, September 2007.

Fougere, Barbara, BSCBVMS, "Pet Sage: Reducing Canine Obesity," *www.petsage.com*.

Hawks, Bill, "Organic Pet Food Task Force," April 7, 2006, *www.ams.usda.gov/nosb/meetings/OrgPetFood.pdf*.

Holve, Jean, DVM, "Pet Food Regulation," *www.littlebigcat.com*.

Kawczynska, Claudia, "Trust the Hand That Feeds You," *Bark*, May/June 2007.

Keith, Christie, "The Whole(istic) Truth about Pet Food," "Are Raw Meat and Dairy Products Safe?" and "Natural Diet: Don't Just Do It," *www.caberfeidh.com*.

Martin, Ann, excerpt from *Foods Pets Die For*, New Sage Press, 1997; "Polluted Pet Food," *Nexus*, December 1996.

Nash, Holly, DVM, MS, "Food Standards by AAFCO," and "Feline Hepatic Lipidosis," *www.peteducation.com*.

National Research Council, "Estimated Caloric Intake for Dogs," and "Estimated Daily Caloric Intake for Cats," www.nationalacademies.org/nrc.

Natural Pet Systems, "Barf Diet Specifics," and "Ingredients and Analysis," *www.barkproducts.com*.

Nestle, Marion, "Eating Made Simple," *Scientific American*, September 2007.

Pearl, Mary C., "Better Planet: Antibiotic Use on the Farm," *Discover*, September 2007.

Pet Food Institute, "The Pet Food Report," and "What Is PFI?" *www.petfoodinstitute.org*.

Spielman, Bari, DVM, "Megaesophagus in Dogs," PetPlace.com, *www.petplace.com*.

Syufy, Franny, "About Cats: Before You Try a Raw Food Diet," *www.cats.about.com*.

Tri-Natural Products, Inc., "Ingredients," *www.trinatural.com*.

Tyson, John, "Pet & Products: Life Stages," *Pet Business*, July 2007.

Veterinary Pet Insurance, "Pet Obesity Costing Millions," August 16, 2007, *http://press.petinsurance.com/pressroom/index.cfm?prid=222*.

Virginia Cooperative Extension, "A Consumer Guide to Safe Handling of Raw Meat," Publication 458-016, October 1996.

Volhard, Wendy, "Natural Diet Foundation," *www.volhard.com/holistic*.

Wikipedia, "Escherichia coli," *www.wikipedia.org*.

Woolf, Norma Bennett, "Dog Owners Guide: Obesity in Dogs," and "Building a Balanced Diet," *www.canismajor.com*.

Index